Rebooting Social Studies

Rebooting Social Studies

Strategies for Reimagining History Classes

Greg Milo

ROWMAN & LITTLEFIELD
Lanham • Boulder • New York • London

Published by Rowman & Littlefield
A wholly owned subsidiary of The Rowman & Littlefield Publishing Group, Inc.
4501 Forbes Boulevard, Suite 200, Lanham, Maryland 20706
www.rowman.com

Unit A, Whitacre Mews, 26-34 Stannary Street, London SE11 4AB

British Library Cataloguing in Publication Information Available

Library of Congress Cataloging-in-Publication Data

Library of Congress Cataloging-in-Publication Data Available

978-1-4758-2875-7 (cloth : alk. paper)
978-1-4758-2876-4 (pbk. : alk. paper)
978-1-4758-2877-1 (electronic)

♾ ™ The paper used in this publication meets the minimum requirements of American
National Standard for Information Sciences Permanence of Paper for Printed Library
Materials, ANSI/NISO Z39.48-1992.

Printed in the United States of America

Contents

Preface

Just a Teacher

I've got a question for you. What does society expect from its teachers?

    a. Challenge students to mentally grow through high expectations?
    b. Model the ethical standards that will help strengthen soft skills?
    c. Create experiences for students that are relevant to their future careers?
    d. Guide them in the art of articulating a position that is supported with facts?
    e. All of the above and more?

Society places in the hands of teachers the future of their children and the overall success of society. That's quite the responsibility, and teachers happily embrace that challenge.

But can we trust these teachers with our children? Seems like society is on the fence. They're just teachers, right?

Go ahead and Google "just a teacher" and see what you find. There's no doubt a prevailing sense across the country that teachers are *just* teachers, and even if you don't agree with that statement, there is a belief among teachers that others see or treat them as *just* teachers.

Such a mindset is detrimental for teachers and especially students.

Simply put, when people don't feel respected, they tend not to do their job to the fullest. It seems counterproductive to treat teachers as *just* teachers.

Teachers are far from second-rate professionals who settle for an occupation that rewards them with the bonus every summer of lounging poolside.

On the contrary, teachers are creative and adaptable—the embodiment of necessary twenty-first-century skills.

In fact, society could stand to benefit from realizing all that teachers have to offer and putting the talents of teachers to use for the greater community.

If teachers are seen as *just teachers*, then it makes their job of being creative innovators much more difficult. If teachers are not given the respect of possessing the skills of adaptability and thinking on their tippy-toes, then it limits their ability to be seen as players who can bridge the classroom to the surrounding community. If teachers are seen as people who teach because they can't do "real work," then teachers will never be looked at as having answers on how to reform and improve education.

Would you ask someone you didn't respect for advice on how to help you build a new deck for your house? Probably not. The same goes for teachers. Just as a carpenter wants to use his tools to build your deck, a teacher wants to provide children with the tools necessary to think critically. Makes sense, right?

However, would you ask a teacher to be your new creative consultant? Why not?

What does a teacher know about developing strategic ways to reach an audience, you ask? A lot.

Would you hire a teacher to be your event planner? Why not?

Every day teachers plan events for an audience. The events have to be meaningful, engaging, and diverse, and it stands a good chance that some of the teacher's audience doesn't even want to be at their event, whether it's in the classroom or on a field trip, so the teacher has to work especially hard to get everyone of the students to buy in to the event.

Would you hire a teacher to be your press secretary? Why not?

Most every day, teachers have to field difficult questions and structure meaningful answers and messages that satisfy an audience.

Go ahead. Google *other jobs for teachers* and see what you get. You see a range of other jobs associated with teaching.

Simply put, there exists a damaging teacher image problem. And it is our job as teachers to change this image shortcoming.

Let's change the image. When the news says that teachers are failing or are paid too much, let's counter that with all that we do. We need to think of ourselves as key contributors to society. And we need to keep building our skills to remain relevant and vital to the next generation. We hear a lot of voices putting us down, but we know it's not true, but we also have to make an effort to prove it. Let's show society what we're made of!

TWELVE AWESOME TEACHER TRAITS

Something we need to learn straight away: teachers are pretty awesome, and they have an awesome responsibility. We need to keep our confidence and inspiration. Those two things can carry us a long way, but it's a mindset game. If we let the negativity sink in and fill our minds, there won't be much room for positive inspiration and confidence.

Let's run down the necessary traits of a good teacher—kind of build a resume together

1. Creative: A teacher has to keep the attention of the students, and that can't be done with the same stale flow each day. A teacher has to keep the students off-guard, always on their toes, and this is done through creative lessons that aren't anchored in textbooks. You want to look at an old idea in a new way? Ask a teacher.

2. Adaptable: Teachers are required to build curriculums and lessons, but no matter how much planning is done, some wrench will fall, and the teacher will quickly have to find a new path to the objective. This is not an easy skill to master, and some people just can't do it. Whether it's a sudden change in the daily schedule, or a fire drill sounds, or you just realize that your class hasn't a clue about the point of the week-long lesson you taught, the number of "Whoa, I got to think of something fast" moments are many in the teaching world.

3. Patient: Teachers can't really discriminate between who they want to be patient with and who they want to ignore. Nope. Teachers have to cater to the needs of all of their students, those who want to be there and those who don't; those who excel and those who struggle. Each day has to be differentiated to address the needs of each student.

4. Communicator: Not many jobs require you to be "on stage" every work day, presenting information in a manner that is comprehensible to the future of America. Monday morning? You're presenting. Not feeling well? You're presenting. Personal problem? You're presenting. Not only are teachers always on call to be the personality in the classroom, but they are responsible for finding ways to relay information to the students in a way that is enjoyable and memorable.

5. Facilitator: Teachers guide students and give them the tools necessary to master the lessons on their own. The job of a teacher isn't just to shove content down the throat of the students. Nope. Instead, the goal is to teach skills so that the students become self-reliant. The question becomes: When do you act like the mama bird and let the students fly on their own?

6. Model: Like politicians running for office, there isn't much room for teachers to be mistake-ridden humans. Teachers are looked to by their

students, by their school, by their students' parents, and by their administration to be model citizens. It's difficult to accept hearing on the news that your teacher calls on a certain population to be deported, but it seems normal for a politician to do so. You don't expect to hear about your son's teacher talking nasty about students while hidden in the depths of the teachers' lounge, but it's fine for gossip to be the theme of a television program you and your son watch. Heck, it's strange enough for a student to see her teacher at the grocery store carrying a six-pack of beer, even if the student's father has a case at home in the fridge.

7. Leader: A teacher is a leader in the community, a leader for the students, and a leader in knowledge. There's Teachers of the Year, Teachers Who Make a Difference, Teachers Who Go Above and Beyond—these are the teachers who are appreciated, and who people comment, "Now that person is really making a difference." Students look up to teachers as people to emulate—"I want to be like them." Teachers are expert in their field of study, and people turn to the Social Studies teachers when they have a question about history.

8. Innovation: Teachers consistently must come up with new methods to excite and gain the attention of the students. Teachers have to embrace new technological trends. Teachers have to develop lessons, projects, and programs that speak to the changing generations. An innovative lesson five years ago doesn't quite fly today. Teachers recognize their audience and build lessons that speak to the interest of that audience—if they don't, they run the risk of losing their students.

9. Multidimensional: Teachers teach, contribute to committees geared toward improving the school, select texts and supplementary readings, build websites, organize calendars and future events, show their spirit and support of the student body, write recommendations, attend conferences and workshops and seminars, take classes for professional development, present to other educators, plan school trips (domestic and international), drive the school van, promote their school to aspiring students and parents, lead professional learning communities, mentor younger teachers, and a bunch of other stuff they're called upon to do on a moment's notice.

10. Altruistic: A teacher's entire existence is consumed by the drive to help others succeed. Teachers gauge their success based on that one student who comes back to high school years after graduating to thank his teacher for doing their job.

11. Content expert: Teachers keep up with educational best practice, but they also keep up to date with their content—in this case, Social Studies. History teachers capture the imagination of their students when they tell rich, detailed, personal stories about people and events.

Bottom line, history teachers nerd-out on their subject, reading books and researching historical events. History teachers travel to historical spots, like the ruins on Delos or the remnants of the trenches of World War I or the museums of DC. We are nerds, and we love to excite our students about what excites us.

12. Marketer: Teachers *sell* their classes, their clubs, their extracurricular activities, their field trips—lots of stuff. They contact their local media to get their students and programs some recognition. They promote their programs in order to get funding and keep them rolling.

Genuine Social Studies teachers try their best at all of the twelve traits. Sure, sometimes a teacher might let one trait slide, and there are those days where teachers have to throw their hands up and plead for a reset, but overall, the committed teachers go through the grind of addressing the twelve traits as best they can.

The collection of stories and projects included in the following pages are intended to ignite action. Use these chapters to spark an idea that you can enhance and make your own. Allow these chapters to spark questions, conversations, and debate.

Through my thirteen years teaching high school Social Studies, I came to believe that there's plenty that needs to be refigured. After a couple of years, I reflected on the overall curriculum and activities and realized I was bored with the usual, which probably meant my students were bored, too. I sat at my desk and looked out onto a crowd of students busy filling in blank spaces on a handout taken from the text. It was an energy-killer.

What's the point? I wondered. And when I realized that the point was to prepare students for an ever-changing, complicated world, I concluded that I needed to take a stand.

Do we want students filling in blanks or creating the blanks? Do we want students choosing the correct response or creating the various responses? Do we want students sitting in organized rows or designing the rows?

Let's light some dynamite and reduce what we think to be true to ashes, and then we can reboot our discipline with a refreshing and relevant angle.

DYNAMITE

I collaborated with a teacher to create a new program where we took students out each week to hang out with the homeless. We wanted to challenge the students to engage by placing them in a reality that is often ignored.

Another colleague and I created overseas experiences for our students that would place them face to face with international leaders and organizations.

We wanted our students to take what they learned from people whom they spoke with and interpret it into something that could teach others.

I created new courses that focused on students choosing their own topics, getting outside the school building, and analyzing and critiquing multiple perspectives.

I quit relying on traditional textbooks, and I decided to start making my own student companions.

I pushed tests aside and started developing creative and engaging project-based assessments that required my students to engage and improve multiple skills.

I wanted students moving around and working together and designing solutions and then redesigning better solutions.

There's nothing uniform about what students will encounter as they prepare for their careers. Whether they weld pipes or cure diseases or teach high school, students will be expected to approach a problem from multiple lenses.

BUCKING THE SYSTEM

Bucking the system was never easy. Students had to adapt to my style of teaching, and I had to keep pushing back against the status quo.

If more and more teachers buck the system, the system might eventually get the message.

There are plenty of conferences out there that teach teachers new ideas, but I'm going to guess that the best ideas come straight from teachers. You have innovative ideas that can help improve education. Some of the most exciting and energizing stuff I've heard has come from speaking one on one with another teacher. So teachers, let's start talking and sharing those good ideas, and guess what, you can save yourself from having to pay a conference entrance fee.

WHAT'S AT STAKE?

Continuing down a road, this road, is detrimental to our students' future and, therefore, society's future. If we focus on preparing students to memorize hundreds (if not thousands) of years of history, we're selling the world short.

Let's restructure our Social Studies courses so that students spend more time analyzing specific events. Allow students to dig deep. Allow the event to tell a story. Investigate characters. Extend beyond the classroom and engage with society. Present students with the realities of their community.

It's time to prepare our students to solve our problems, fill our jobs, fix our neighborhoods, and that won't be done by glossing over thousands of years of world history.

Acknowledgments

Thank you to my supportive wife, Terra, who encouraged me to take on the challenge of writing this book, despite the many other projects that already kept me from giving my home 100 percent of my attention. I'd like to thank my mom and dad for structuring an inquisitive and creative environment for little Greg and his brothers, which placed an infectious bug in me to always dig deeper from many directions.

Special thanks to Dr. Mary Anne Beiting for reading through my manuscript and suggesting I remove the term "kick-ass," among other strengthening edits. Similarly, thanks to Brad Scott and Anthony Boarman for giving the manuscript another set of eyes.

To my creative friends and educators who I collaborated with on some of the example projects and lessons in this book, especially Micah Kraus, Jason Horinger, Matt Bryant, and Kevin Taylor.

I have to express my gratitude to editor, Sarah Jubar, as well as Bethany Janka and the people at Rowman & Littlefield for suggesting I write this book and happily assisting me along the way.

Finally, thanks to Akron Coffee Roasters for keeping me caffeinated during this project.

Introduction

It's December 2015. The Ohio Department of Education just issued the newest change to the state Social Studies requirements—the newest new one. This time, schools must be sure students leave high school with a minimum of a semester of World History, which, based on the state standards, is AD 1600 to the present.

Just as a refresher, the World History class goes a little something like this: students learn about the philosophies of Hobbes and Locke. They celebrate their own heritage by cheering on the American Revolution. Students examine the powers of the Enlightenment and its impact on France and how it and nationalism led to later revolutions. Students will scribble notes about capitalism and the Industrial Revolution into notebooks. Then they'll get to World War I and II, and the Cold War.

And on, and on, and on.

This is the course all high school students endure.

Snore.

History is rich and abundant. It includes thousands of years and miles. It is a struggle of perspectives and realities. There are no absolutes. It's not black or white. It's both!

It's the unknown that makes history something to study, something to ponder and debate. It's a subject made by examination and deliberation. There are no simple equations.

As a member of the Social Studies curriculum, history analyzes society, the behavior and decisions of people. History includes a study of the rational as well as irrational.

It's a blast—if done right.

But history can also put students to sleep if it seems distant or lacks soul.

History can be quite exhausting. Heck, it's everything that has ever happened, everywhere—that's a lot stuff. Given that fact, how do we select what our students should learn? Can history be portioned in a to-go box? And why do we demand our students learn this history stuff? What's the point? Is it to remember the past for the sake of posterity? Or, is the study of history not so straightforward—perhaps not the exciting, motivating, and energizing kind?

The study of history is about the struggle to wrestle with the puzzles of the world. The study of history assists students in building their problem-solving skills. It's true that there is no set answer in studying human behavior, but if students practice the critical thinking skills that accompany an analysis of historical events, students can improve their decision-making skills and build a repertoire of abstract thought.

But despite the complex ambiguity of World History, the traditional curriculum and national standards try desperately to build structure and borders and timeframes and eras, all answerable with an A or B or C or all of the above.

What if Social Studies took advantage of and embraced its wealth of diversity?

Too scary?

If we didn't mandate a timeframe, would students have a common learning experience? How would high schools know what incoming freshmen learned? And aren't there just milestones in history we should all learn?

Let's take a couple steps back.

WHAT'S IN A TIMEFRAME?

Why is a particular timeframe mandated? What is the significance of this stretch from 1600 to 2016? Why not 1700? High school students aren't required to learn anything before 1600 because it is believed they have already learned that in junior high school.

Whether or not students remember their seventh-grade World History course, they will be required to start their high school Social Studies career in AD 1600. That's not really the issue. Students and teachers can pick up history in any year and build sense around it.

But let's consider this imperative 1600-to-present World History course. It basically goes like this: Britain and France do a lot of rad stuff. Later they're joined on the continent by Austria, Prussia (not yet Germany), and Russia. These countries mess about a bit with other regions of the world. Then nationalism turns everything upside down, until there's big war, where Europe bashes itself in the face over and over again—we call this World War I, followed by another war, more horrific than the first. Then, the United States enters and dominates, along with the Soviet Union. Ultimately, the

Soviet Union turns back into Russia (a very confusing concept for students), and the 1600-to-present course ends with the United States trying to hold the world together—very worldly.

It's supposed to be a survey class. A survey course is best described as the relaying of hundreds of years of events from the teacher to the student with the hopes that something will spark interest in the student.

But what is history? Is it 1600 to 2016? In our increasingly interrelated world, is a focus on events leading to the creation and rise of the United States really benefiting anyone? Let's remember, high school students will gain a pretty strong understanding of America's greatness in their mandated 1877-to-present U.S. History course.

Since it is so broad, must we give parameters for world history? If there are no timeframes that all teachers stick to, how could all the students learn the same stuff? How could a kid change high schools and not feel lost? What stuff do we really want our students to learn?

Does our obsession with eras accomplish what we want it to accomplish? (And what is it we want to accomplish, exactly?)

It's no secret that Social Studies is moving away from memorizing historical facts. The programs that don't move away from that antiquated system risk sending their graduating seniors to college ill-prepared.

It's also no secret that employers are looking for young people who can adapt, communicate, and problem solve, all while doing so creatively.

Social Studies programs that are interested in preparing their students for the future must have the so-called twenty-first-century skills in mind, but are twenty-first-century skills era-specific? Nope. None of them include a specific historic timeframe.

Any era will do. Any event will do.

If the goal is to help students hone and sharpen these "skills for the future," it makes sense to toss the traditional view of Social Studies out the window and run far away, without looking back. Forget the mandated courses that cover hundreds of years, or even thousands.

Instead, perhaps topical studies are more suited for the development of skills needed for the future.

BEYOND THE BLACK AND WHITE

There's a lot of juicy stuff in a 1600-to-present class, but do we miss the juice by covering so much? Do we ever actually remove the peel and rip into the good stuff?

There are so many great stories to be told in history, so let's tell them like stories.

Very few interesting stories have no main character, cover hundreds of years, shift from plot to plot endlessly, and have no end (or start, for that matter).

To our students, this is the equivalent of a lengthy black and white film: think *Citizen Kane*.[1]

Not only does the traditional World History course fail to provide students the time needed to focus and develop twenty-first-century skills, but it's also boring.

So how do we address the skills and make it interesting?

One possible answer would be fewer, more in-depth topics during the course of a semester, where students are introduced to reality-based learning, such as taking on the role of a character during a given event or era. Or perhaps each quarter could embody its own theme, such as the Treaty of Versailles, allowing students to enter that world and really get a taste for it.

"But wait," says the critic, "do we really want to send students to college without a good base? If we just teach our students four topics over the course of a semester, they won't be introduced to dozens of important topics."

True, students will be introduced to fewer historical events, but is that such a bad thing?

If a World History course is a true World History course, that's *a lot* of stuff. As mentioned, that's everything that's ever happened, ever. Who's to decide what the most important events in history are?

Let's allow students time to ponder and dig and truly understand history and make it relevant. This can be accomplished with fewer topics over the course of a semester or quarter.

LET'S FOCUS

Is 1600-to-present focused? Does it allow students time to really dig deep into an event and understand the people, the mood, the perspectives? Is it relevant? Can students really understand or empathize with those involved in the 1605 Gunpowder Plot when the topic is introduced and completed in twenty minutes? And why not use 1605 to examine the reign of Akbar the Great of the Mughal Empire? Which story is more important? Is either more important than the other? Is one more important to U.S. students? Is a focus on Britain really worldly, or does it actually restrict our students' understanding and appreciation of the world?

Narrowing the mandated study might prove more fruitful. What if the state mandated a course that examined 1914 to 2015? More focused, yes. Plenty of juicy stuff to mess around with. The narrative could be quite simple: the events of World War I and the decisions afterward lead to our current instability.

What if teachers could select their own four topics or two topics over a semester or a quarter—topics they're totally jazzed about and can become experts in and lead their students into really entering that world?

Over the course of twelve years, students are intermittently presented with facts from ancient Sumer to ISIS, much of which doesn't translate as they learn a little about the story in fifth grade, a little more in seventh and the rest in ninth grade.

Why not just a ninth-grade course called From Sumer to ISIS? Now that's a course! Focused and relevant.

World History texts move quickly from chapter to chapter, nicely compartmentalizing historic events into watered-down slices in an attempt to calm mental digestion. But in the process, depth is lost, as is understanding. Further, excitement is lost, and a study of doldrums puts kids to sleep.

The traditional historical eras used by textbook publishers to create chapters and units also give the false impression of history being a collection of nicely packaged events. We love packages. Receiving packages at Christmas are quite the exciting joy, but in the historical sense, leading students through a series of "eras" creates a false sense of history.

Also, covering dozens of eras makes it difficult to examine just how complicated the "eras" actually are. Instead, students end with a very structured understanding of history. I call it the "Math Problem." The Math Problem is when students are taught that the study of historical events resembles a mathematical equation, where the solution is the same no matter the scenario —the history repeats itself fallacy.

We can escape this lack of depth and myth of the Math Problem by investigating fewer "eras" more deeply.

WHO DO WE WANT PARTICIPATING?

We shouldn't assume the current education system will last forever. There's online courses and dual credit opportunities for students to go about their education à la carte. Let's take a step and consider some alternatives for the future that might make students' history classes engaging, active, and applicable for the twenty-first century.

There's a line in the National Social Studies Standards that reads, "learners are influenced by the social and intellectual environments in which they find themselves." This is totally true, which is why we need to take efforts to expand that environment beyond the classrooms. The national standards also stress that the main purpose of Social Studies is to prepare students for participation in society.

If Social Studies focus on the goal of forming critical thinkers through an array of engaging and real-life experiences, it can rebrand itself as an exciting high school discipline that inspires students to further their studies in history. Students will see the Indiana Jones in the museum curators or the *Madam Secretary* in international studies, rather than as a path toward a drab life as a struggling History major.

There's plenty to complain about in education, but for the purpose of this book, we'll keep that stuff in the teachers' lounge, where all the intrigue and plotting occurs. The majority of this book will offer alternatives to the norms—both big ideas that require a restructuring of education and small, quick fixes that can be easily implemented into a current lesson. Hopefully, something within will spur a conversation or spark an idea that helps guide history into the future.

So, how do we deconstruct the doldrums? Here's a quick glimpse of the chapters within:

Chapter 1. Let's take a moment to listen to students. What do they appreciate? How do they learn best? A diverse collection of high schoolers and recent graduates speak frankly about their education.

Chapter 2. What is the focus of school? What's the point? What do we want the students to get out of these hours upon hours of time spent studying? Do we even know? Does the content sometimes get in the way of the point? Perhaps courses like World History spend too much time concerned with content.

Chapter 3. Select fewer topics to really chew apart. Set aside the breadth, the rush to get through all of the material in a year, and take a moment to decide what two or three topics you could ask your class to research, inside and out. Rather than the rush of information, readjust your students' brains to appreciate the slow and concentrated world of depth. To do so, however, you'll have to debug those young brains.

Chapter 4. Courses, such as World History, have essentially been the same for generations. Chapter after chapter, students take notes and tests. Can we develop a new approach? Can we look at these historic chapters in a different way? Try developing themes to carry you through the year—something the students can use as a comfortable guide. Can you bring current events into the chapters to help make them relevant for the students? Can you bring up the rights of refugees, migrant workers, or militias when discussing the liberty of the Enlightenment?

Chapter 5. It also should be understood that no idea is perfect, especially the first time around. Some of the ideas in this book might work for you and some might not, and not all of the ideas will work the same for each teacher, or look the same. And sometimes, an idea, whether it's found in this book or conceived on your own, will flop, but schools and teachers have to be willing to take chances, as scary as that is.

Chapter 6. Build independent studies that place the ownership in the hands of the students. Can they develop and run their own business? It takes some work and lobbying, but creating new courses and pitching them to the administration also helps move this stagnant industry into the future. Try working with a local university to implement a dual credit course, or create a course that is based in community engagement and introduces students to career opportunities. Give students the opportunity to hear about future employment possibilities—a sort of career audit. Apprenticeships in Germany have attracted plenty of attention in the States as a means to provide students with experiences they can take with them into the workforce.

Chapter 7. Organizing trips overseas isn't easy. Making them meaningful and attaching them to a course curriculum is even more difficult, but it's entirely fruitful. You want to give your International Politics class a chance to study the ethnic tensions in Kosovo? Do it! Pack up those bags and go. Make it happen! Need some funding? We can tackle that one, too.

Chapter 8. Toy with the idea of an à la carte system where students can select from a variety of choices. Sure, there's the mandated curriculum, but student-selected independent studies on top of the tested curriculum can motivate and bring the class to life. A history course titled Human Rights Not Revenge focuses students' attention and allows for deep inquiry. If a kid doesn't find that interesting, she could always choose a course called Terrorism: Here, There, and Everywhere. A course on sports teams' nicknames? Why not?

When thinking long term, consider pushing for alternative schedules. Why are classes offered only during the traditional school day? Disrupt tradition for the sake of our students by developing electives that are scheduled after the school day or over the summer.

Chapter 9. Time. All of these idealistic propositions take time to develop. Schools must be willing to invest in not just teachers' professional development but also time to allow teachers to see their PD and ideas through. Our school system is awash in mandated requirements that cut into teachers' time. Learn how a veteran teacher makes the most of his limited time to think.

Inspiration needs time, and teachers need time, either in professional learning communities or independently, to brainstorm an idea and see it through to the end. Don't be afraid to start your own PLC outside of school. When "off duty," share ideas with teachers from other schools in a casual setting—make it fun.

Chapter 10. We need a mindset shift, the Big Why. Let's make a positive difference. Often, progressive educators point to Finland as the jewel of education, but this gem didn't happen in an instant, and it took an agreed upon shift. Consider the original reason you wanted to teach. Ponder that reason and emotion, and use that to manifest the positive change. It'll take work, and it takes the right environment. We can do this team! We can shift Social Studies in our favor. Finland did.

Chapter 11. Build a book or link up with a local publication to get your students' work in print and seen. Rather than use the course exam as the endpoint, make it a class project, where the students work as a team to create something they can show prospective colleges. On top of asking your students to build a text from class content, you too could build a text tailored to the needs of your students. A good summer spent collecting the best resources for your students could prove more resourceful than any $100 textbook.

Whatever that week has in store or whatever the students want to experience—build a program that takes students outside of the school environment on a weekly basis and into the community. Even if it's confined to the classroom, provide students with opportunities to experience. Include a mission or morality or character-building component with the excursion and you have something that's bound to be funded by alumni or the community.

We don't have to wait for the future. Let's work with what we have now. While the prevailing system of education isn't going away anytime soon, there's no reason to toss our hands up in defeat. Educators, stand and deliver! Teachers can work with the mandated curriculum and make it feel less rigid, motivating teachers and students alike. Embedding a course with engaging projects that place the students in the driver's seat provide students with real-life experiences and challenges that ultimately strengthen critical thinking and creativity skills necessary for their future careers. Sprinkle a course with experiential learning, project-based activities, and reality-based lessons and watch the class come to life.

NOTE

1. Forgive my blast of *Citizen Kane*. I'm a fan, but I'm guessing many high school students wouldn't give it a chance. However, I've shown *Gunga Din* to classes during the unit on imperialism. I explained to the students ahead of time to embrace the 1939 campiness and enjoy it. Laugh at it even, but take the time to extract those characteristics of imperialism we discussed. In the end, most of the students enjoy it. I've even had students tell me it was the best movie they've ever seen in school. Heck, I used to watch it when I was sick at home from school.

Chapter One

Horror Stories and Happy Stories

Students tend to be left out of the conversation when it comes to what works and what doesn't in education. Maybe this is because they're "just kids" and "adults know better." Maybe this is because each student is different, making it difficult to publish a one-size-fits-all book. Whatever the reasoning is, students' opinions don't seem to matter when it comes to education. But they should.

Groves and Welsh (2010) write, "Students hold favourable views toward learning and school when they are participants in activities and experiences that are meaningful and interesting, and which provide opportunities to succeed both academically and developmentally."

Further, in 2014, Grant Wiggins wrote a series of blog posts about the fact that the high school structure is resistant to reform, and that the resistance hurt student achievement. A list of Wiggins's findings was posted on the blog *Teach Thought*. One of the many points listed was that students learn best when the teacher "has us do work hands on and with more discussion." The students didn't learn best when completing what they believed to be busy work.

This book isn't ENIGMA. It doesn't have a money-back guarantee. It's not a cure-all remedy. Some students might even deplore the suggestions in this book, but the contents have been inspired based on feedback from students—what they have enjoyed and learned from.

This chapter includes a series of student reflections and interviews, casual conversations, and actual assignments.

The attempt was to pull from an array of abilities (from only the high school where I taught): lower-achievers, higher-achievers, freshmen, alumni, students who enjoy school, and students who just plain hate it.

1

Why start the book with the voice of students? Because those voices matter most.

STUDENTS' SHARE

One student spent her spring break working in New Orleans's 9th Ward, eleven years after Hurricane Katrina. When asked about her experience, she spoke passionately and eloquently. She explained about FEMA markings on the sides of buildings used for search and rescue. *You hear about it on TV is one thing, but then you go and do it, and it's completely different. I had researched it online before going, but when you see it . . . at that point it becomes real.*

Real. The learning experience was real. Julia was involved, on the front lines. What spoke most to her was being in the action—the virtual research lacked something. What about other real, engaging experiences?

Jessica was part of the first team (we called them The Pioneers) of students who joined us into the unknown with a new way to get students actively learning and engaged in community responsibility. Project HOPE began in 2009. The idea was not an original one, but the inspiration was that the school was lacking some active expression of social justice, so campus ministry and Social Studies joined forces and ran with what would become a popular experience for students, despite it being a rather unpolished experiential learning opportunity. Now early in her career with the *Washington Post*, Jessica wrote these words for this book:

Every Wednesday started the same. The sound of crinkling of aluminum foil filled Hoban's basement cafeteria as busy hands wrapped sandwiches for delivery. The idea for Project HOPE was fairly simple: we'd take these sandwiches and snacks, hop in a van, and find the people who needed them.

If this was like any "service" experience I'd had before, we would have set up our operation somewhere and asked the people in need to come to us. We would have passed those sandwiches from behind a folding table. We'd smile, and say hi—but not make any real connections. Like reading a textbook, we would see hardship, but only from afar.

In Project HOPE, the students followed the sandwiches into the van and followed the sandwiches out of the van. After we passed out the food, we stayed to talk, listen, and learn.

We met the mom who woke up with a cough, and a few weeks later was racked in medical bills out of her control. We met an elderly man who grew up just a few streets away from my house. And a twenty-something who looked as young as we did. Sometimes we talked about the heartbreaking problems that led them to that day. Sometimes we just talked about how ketchup is really, really good.

With each conversation, this group of sheltered teenagers came closer to the realization that the people who needed the sandwiches were not so different than the people who wrapped them.

This experience helped lead me to my job today, as a features reporter at the Washington Post. *The stories I love writing the most are the ones where I get to bring readers closer to people who are different than them. So often, we hear about events in the news, but don't stop to consider what life is like for the people whose lives will change if that bill is passed, policy is implemented, or problem isn't solved. Pausing to meet and understand those people—by serving them sandwiches or by reading their stories—is how we begin to see what we have in common. And how can we make the world better, if we don't all realize that we're in this place together?*

I am forever grateful to have learned that lesson at a time when I was figuring out what I was meant to do in life.

Christina wanted an experience where she could learn about a specific topic that interested her. She wanted a challenge, but not something that was merely preparing her for a test. She wanted a course that was preparing her for her career, and she wanted that course to be focused on international politics.

Christina wrote: *The adoption of International Politics as a dual credit course gave me the opportunity to learn about topics I was extremely interested in, but did not think I would get the chance to learn about until college. It was easily my favorite course, and I looked forward to the class each and every day because of the fascinating article topics and lively Socratic seminars we had. The article discussion gave me the opportunity to not only learn from the text and the teacher but from my fellow students as well.*

Through this class I was able to gain the analytical skills to make sense of lengthy scholarly articles, while also gaining confidence in my ability to speak my opinion and analysis of the text. Instead of reading textbooks cover to cover, I was able view varying opinions on controversial topics, and then formulate my own opinion, rather than blindly accepting what the textbook told me. This class taught me how to be an independent mind, while also working along others as a community of learners, discussing prevalent and pressing issues that face our world today.

International Politics was my first glimpse into college-level coursework and academic rigor. Unlike various AP courses, the dual-credit class exposed me to invaluable skills of document analysis and summarization, two skills that I have used extensively at the College of Wooster. Three of my major classes are formatted in the same structure as the dual-credit class, which has given me a significant advantage over my peers who were not familiar with extensive document analysis.

Tess took Christina's point a step further when she connected the International Politics course to her experience in Kosovo, where students saw the course in real life.

I wanted a challenge. I needed a challenge. And, a dual-credit class gave me that opportunity. In my junior year of high school, I took a newly intro-duced class International Politics. The class would be tougher in regard to workload and concepts, but, through St. Louis University, it was also dual-credit.

On top of pushing me academically, this class, similar to college-level classes, went more in--depth into a specific field. I did not just learn interna-tional politics, I was immersed in it. We had multiple, deep academic read-ings on various topics, which we then dissected in class discussions, applying concepts of international politics to current events.

Class did not end in school but physically became global when I, along with some peers, went on a ten-day photojournalistic trip to Kosovo. I was no longer just learning international politics, I was living it, watching abstract concepts become concrete. In just ten days, I absorbed more than I could ever learn in a semester in class.

Now, studying government and economics at Cornell University, I recog-nize the passion the international politics class ignited within me, not just for the subject but for active learning.

Katie talked about how her favorite classes were those where she gets to interact with the subject. *I liked when we read about something and then we experience it. It puts more value on what you've read. I also like being able to speak face to face with experts of the topic we're studying.* Katie was referring to a project where she had to interview people in the community to complete her research and thesis. She enjoyed learning from others who were actually working in the city because it *showed what could be done in the community.*

In fact, she was actually offered a job during one of the interviews she was conducting.

Similar to Katie, Austin enjoyed the interactive experiences. *I liked hearing from the speakers in class, because you got to hear straight from an expert and hear about the nitty gritty details and visual anecdotes.* Austin specifi-cally referenced a marine who spoke to the class about Afghanistan and Iraq. *The personal story of war and the first hand experiences of war really put U.S. foreign policy into perspective, much more than the text.*

Speshal didn't always get along with her education. High school wasn't really her favorite thing for several reasons, but one of them would have been what she considered to be just a bunch of boring subjects to study. She was kind enough to write some thoughts. She specifically references a class called Hometown Histories where the class learns about, well, their hometown: Akron, Ohio. The following is straight from an email from Speshal.

Mr. Milo's Hometown Histories class wasn't what I expected it to be. I expected some long overdramatic story of how Akron's long boring history is what makes Akron the best city, not necessarily expecting vocalized truth of the statement. I thought I was going to be assigned a big text book, titled Akron *and be forced to read such a bland book and be quizzed on Akron's history. But I was badly mistaken. Mr. Milo brought in speakers, what seemed like every other week, to speak about the different opportunities happening in Akron and what makes Akron so unique. We were taken on field trips around Akron and actually had fun learning what we couldn't have learned inside a classroom. Mr. Milo was able to divert the mindset of everyday overdrawn learning and make it carelessly enjoyable knowledge.*

Jason Segedy and the neighborhoods is [sic] what stuck most. I felt like I learned the most interesting stuff from him simply because it drew me in. I like that he had ideas for the neighborhoods and was able to give examples of what our neighborhoods could be like. I also remember the Better Block's purpose and ideas and what they could do for neighborhoods. I liked the goal of the Better Block because they want to promote local businesses. I liked how they went into communities to show what they could be like. That all stuck with me.

I enjoyed the class and recommend it to students who learn better hands on and want to learn about something schools don't teach.

The following is a list of questions and answers for high school graduate Hallie.

What experiential learning opportunities did you participate in while in high school?

In high school I participated in Project HOPE and the Honduras Medical Immersion Trip.

How did the experiential learning enhance your understanding and motivation, if at all?

These experiences were not only the highlights of my time in high school but are still to this day extremely relevant in my life. Just recently in an internship interview, I was able to draw on my experience with Project HOPE as an example of previous experience working/interacting with people of low socioeconomic backgrounds. As far as motivation, I would probably venture to say that these opportunities were the catalysts of my drive to serve and help others with my career in social work. The Honduras trip, which was my first time out of the United States, really opened me up to an entire new world (literally) and shaped my goals for the future. I constantly refer to these experiences as the major influences of my worldview and the foundation of what I believe to be most important.

How did the experiences impact you for the long term?

Before my first time on Project HOPE, and especially before I left for Honduras, I was overcome with apprehension and doubt about what I was about to do. Who was I to go into these situations thinking I had something of real value to offer and that I could actually make an impact? However, I found that after forcing myself to leave this comfort zone that I had never left before, I had the most enriching and fulfilling experiences of my entire life.

Ever since then, in my personal and academic endeavors, I have always actively sought out opportunities and challenges that make me a little nervous. Whether it is studying abroad, volunteering with populations I have never worked with before, reaching out and interviewing for an organization that I would love to work for some day, or simply putting myself out there to meet new people, I try to always stay open and learn as much as I can.

I have found that if I am already comfortable with something, then there isn't room for personal growth. Last year, the week before I left to spend an entire semester studying Spanish in Chile, I had serious reservations about my ability to navigate a city with a population of eight million, about being the only student from Ohio on the trip, and about relating and communicating around the language barrier. Of course, after this initial hesitation, this incredible experiential learning opportunity helped me to challenge myself and to discover parts of myself I never knew before. All of these experiences have helped to expand and shape my worldview and perspective, and it all started with the knowledge and real-life lessons that came along with the experiential learning opportunities I had in high school.

What do you think kept other students from participating in these activities?

I think the most common reason students are hesitant to participate in activities like this is because these opportunities are often seen as extra-curricular and optional. This might be true from a technical perspective, considering these experiences aren't required to graduate or get into college, but the *exposure gained through these experiences is essential for understanding the world around us.*

When I was traveling through Chile, I was surprised at the amount of people from Israel that were traveling all throughout South America. I later learned that every citizen is required to serve for one year in the Israeli military, but before they serve, they are encouraged to take a gap year, see the world, and learn about as many cultures as possible. The reason behind this being that these experiences will make them better soldiers.

I also think there just isn't enough of an emphasis on the importance of these experiences, and many of my friends have expressed to me that they are too overwhelmed with studying for classes and meeting deadlines for projects that they don't have enough time to think about spending extra time engaging with the community or traveling, as valuable and as great it would be to supplement their traditional education with.

Hallie felt compelled to add a few more thoughts:

Our education system is based on grades and percentages, where tests are the key. Do you think this detracts from the educational experience? Or do you know students who were obsessed with the points—placing points above understanding.

I definitely think this detracts from education. Ultimately, in my opinion, there is no way that in five, or even two years, a student will remember the content of every test they nervously crammed for the night before. A real-life experience of engaging in community or global outreach will be something that sticks with a student for their entire life, and I can definitely say that is true for me. I knew so many students in high school and even in college that were so worried and stressed about reaching a certain percentage, that they couldn't even spend time on the subjects they were passionate about.

And, one more bit of student input by sophomore Gracie.

Walking in on the first day of school, after nearly three months of doing absolutely nothing school related, I find myself walking into an elective class called Hometown Histories. I assumed that Hometown Histories would be like a lot of my other classes that followed the seemingly endless cycle of writing notes, completing study guides, taking tests, and cramming for the exam, but we would just study Akron, instead of math or English. Walking into the class, I chose a seat close to the back, placed my notebook on my desk, and waited for the period to begin. When the tardy bell rang and class had begun, my classmates and I waited for some sort of lecture to start, but instead we were just asked to talk about what we knew about Akron. Most of us, thinking we knew so much, said things like "Akron used to be the Rubber Capital of the world" or "Akron was founded in 1825." While we were right, we failed to even mention a fraction of events in Akron's vast and complex history.

I never experienced a standard lecture in Hometown Histories, and I think that's what made the class so successful. As opposed to lecturing, we were taught by articles, pictures, experiences, and speakers about the past, present, and future of Akron. To further the learning we were assigned to research a topic of choice in Akron and to learn about it by going into the community. I focused on the refugee population of Akron and the project lead me everywhere from the library to a Buddhist Temple. Similarly, this class led us everywhere from the John Brown House, the famed abolitionist, to the Akron Art Museum, where we learned about local artists and art initiatives. I was never bored in this class, I was so focused on the experiences that I was gaining, that I didn't even realize how much I learned.

My favorite part about this class was the fact that I could go to the place that I learned about that day and see for myself what it was like. Speakers often came into class to tell us the story of their lives and how Akron played a role in it. I began to realize how unique Akron really was because instead of doing paper homework, our homework was to go out into Akron and explore something new about our city.

As the Hometown Histories progressed, we were again asked a question "what do you know about Akron" by one of our speakers, and the responses changed dramatically from the first time. The answers the class now gave sounded a little something like this:

> *In World War II, the rubber supply was quickly diminishing, as the Axis powers controlled the area where rubber trees were grown. In response, the brightest minds from rubber companies in Akron came together and created what is known as synthetic rubber. This new invention gave the rubber-reliant States the ability to make as much product as necessary, because without rubber, things such as quality tires could have become a luxury, and the war would have been a lot more difficult to win.*

The answers didn't become this in-depth because we were forced to memorize facts; the answers changed because we had changed our mindset on Akron. We realized what a great city Akron is, and how important it was in the past, and how bright the future of Akron is looking. Learning about history was great, but the fact that I was learning so much through the experiences that I had was even better.

After learning in a way that I wasn't staring at a textbook all day, I can honestly say that learning in an engaging way works. Breaking the educational standards causes students to become engaged in what they're learning because it's presented in a new way that we've never experienced before. Hometown Histories focused on the fact that events just don't happen and then 100 years later appear on a page of a history book. Every event from the past shaped the path for something else in the future, and it's really interesting to learn and figure out the connections between things.

I know that it is not possible for every class to become as hands-on as Hometown Histories, but incorporating aspects of the learning style can help students, like me, become curious about what they're learning. Taking Hometown Histories showed me that learning needs to be more than memorizing facts, it needs to be an experience.

CLOSING THOUGHTS

This chapter has been filled with words from students who were known to have been inspired by unconventional education experiences. There are, of course, other students who learn best from lectures and looking over notes and rocking multiple-choice tests. However, consider this: do high test scores inspire active engagement in our democracy?

Chapter Two

What's Missing? Why Do Students Hate History?

"I wish I could take a history class now. I hated it when I was young," said the parent to the teacher.

Do you ever encounter such sadness?

What did they hate about the class? They'll usually say, "It was boring."

What did they find boring about it? They all say something like, "We just had to memorize facts about dead people."

It's hard to argue with that answer. It's a struggle to even memorize the names of the students at the start of each year. Heck, passwords are hard to memorize, and those are used daily.

Memorizing *anything* (names, dates, etc.) isn't very motivating for most people.

- "Class, what year did Benjamin Franklin run away from his brother James?"
- "In what year did Nikita Khrushchev slam his shoe while giving a speech at the UN?"
- "Here, class, memorize the dates of the Thirty Years' War."

Whoa, riveting.

Not to mention that much of what we ask our students to memorize is all very bland—breadth without the depth. Can you imagine if "A long time ago, in a galaxy far, far away . . ." was followed by two hours of generalized paragraphs that glossed over the excitement?

Like dates, content can get in the way of student learning. Does it matter if students memorize the story of Benjamin Franklin—or at least the few things we demand students learn about him? Is it the facts that matter or the *story* that matters?

Content is necessary, no doubt, and dates certainly do give some context to an event so that it fits within the larger story, but have history courses placed too much importance on memorizing content? Does specific content even matter?

WHY DO WE TEACH WHAT WE TEACH?

To have a course, you have to have content. There isn't any doubt about that, but there seems to be a heavy emphasis in our Social Studies standards on content placing information over skills. The assumption by the standards is there's a certain collection of historical events that students must cover in order to be competent in history. Hogwash.

For the state to determine what world history is important for a student to learn hints at a delusion of grandeur. How can anyone in their right mind select *the* historical events for a particular person to study? It's impossible. The fact that the system even attempts to select the events for our history classes just shows its limited knowledge of world history.

"Here, children, study this stuff I learned in high school, whether you're interested or not, because I don't know anything about the rest of the world—seeing as how this is a world history class."

It's ignorance, really. Why are certain sections in a World History text-book lengthier than others? Basically, because the people putting the curriculum together don't know about the other stuff. They didn't grow up learning about pirates in the Mediterranean Sea. They learned about pirates in the Caribbean.

When it comes down to it, there's a battle between content and methods, and methods is losing, even though methods is the more useful of the two—the one that will transform students' minds from recall to that of independence and inquiry.

Which is more important for students to learn: the French Revolution or the Taiping Rebellion? The Victorian Age or the Qajar Age? Perhaps different students in the same class would like to dive into different empires, British or Persian. It might even make for a little fun.

The important question here is whether or not there is a certain core knowledge that history students should learn. For example, should high school students learn about the French Revolution? Or, as history teachers, is it more our responsibility to teach students how to think, whether it's the French Revolution or the Taiping Rebellion?

QUEEN CONTENT

The *problem-solving student* will serve society (and the student) much better in the future than the *date-regurgitator*. A student who has practiced the skills necessary to adapt will more likely innovate than the student who has memorized the events of the Era of Absolutism. [1]

The thinking process must be the focus, not the content. And this can be accomplished with any historical content, from any era and any region of the world.

If education does dethrone Queen Content in favor of a focus on individual thinking skills, education will also have to embrace hands-on, active learning and in-depth, rich inquiry. Schools will have to adopt programs that place students in the driver's seat, working with whatever it is they are studying. Plus, history courses will have to drop the rushed memorize-this-hundreds-of-years mentality and implement topic-specific courses that allow students time to dig through the rigor.

What if the film *Star Wars: A New Hope* was in a history course textbook? What would that look like? Like the Thirty Years' War in a World History course, the film would be only a small part of the overall course, and it might be in a chapter titled "The Galactic Empire" and look a little like this:

> The Galactic Empire had increased its hold on a growing number of planets; however, the rebels continued to fight. In an effort to reign in the rebels, the Empire built a space station that could destroy a planet. In a show of power, the Empire destroyed the planet Alderaan, proving its strength.
>
> The Empire was planning on destroying more planets, which would certainly stall any rebel efforts, but during the Battle of Yavin, rebel pilots found a weakness and the space station was destroyed. This was a damaging blow to the Empire, and it was a huge boost to the rebel morale, but the Empire's growth was merely stalled.

There, that's the movie. That's what we ask students to learn about most wars in history. There are no specific players. There are no personal stories. There isn't much substance. And there's little doubt that the above version of Star Wars would not lead to a series of other movies, action figures, and kids' pajamas.

We love stories that pull us in, stories that don't gloss over the excitement. We are drawn to stories that make us a part of it, that highlight the humanity, that require us to struggle with themes that we can relate to, like right and wrong or good and bad.

Far too often, we model a very hands-off approach to life in the Social Studies. We hand students thick texts that tiptoe over thousands of years of history. Students pass tests by regurgitating the text, and we expect them to be innovative. We give A+ scores for essays that follow the perfect five-paragraph format.

None of this memorizing challenges problem-solving skills or instills moral decision-making. Instead, memorization makes education "a call-and-response game," as a 2013 *Atlantic* article put it. The article written by Ben Orlin goes on to state, "What separates memorization from learning is a sense of meaning."

The meaning has been sapped from the education.

But it's not you! It's the Social Studies—the system that has been in place for years.

So, Social Studies teachers, why do people like history after they leave the clutches of the system? That's the real question.

They like it now because they can read about what interests them. They have a *choice*. They learn about specific stories of specific people. Bottom line—they don't read a textbook and they aren't forced to memorize. They've had more experiences, so they can put meaning to the history.

So, how do we make history interesting now for the students in our classrooms?

Easy. We use our talents as Social Studies teachers to turn the system upside down.

MAKE THE STUDENTS THE EXPERTS

We all know that we have to engage the students and motivate them, but how can we do that given the current system, which sometimes feels stifling or restrictive?

Change takes time, but there are some quick adjustments that can be used now to motivate students. Give the students the tools to **be the expert.** Build in opportunities for the students to physically **move.** Don't be afraid to give them some **independence.**

There are different levels of expertise, and there are different methods to reach expertise. One simple method for a history course is to adjust the content.

The goal of Social Studies is to help encourage participating citizens. That can't be done with reading traditional textbooks, but it can be done with reading supplemental pieces that bring life and humanity to the historical story.

So, is there a quick fix that teachers can implement in their lessons immediately? Yep.

Anything out there that can help with the quick fix?

There are tons of curriculums out there, some good, some bad. One powerful collection is developed by the Choices Program (www.choices.edu).

The curriculum that Choices puts out focuses on world events and history, and it's definitely challenging. Each unit is thoroughly researched and presented in such a way that students can build a strong understanding of events. Choices also includes a focus on values. Their curriculum on human rights challenges students to research a side, reflect on their own view, take a position, and support that decision. It requires students to play a role in the lessons—their own role.

It's one thing to ask students to debate the refugee crisis in Syria, but it's another thing to provide students with the background of specific positions on how to address the crisis and to play that role in a class deliberation. Choices gives you the tools to make this happen.

Choices can be altered for your own purposes. They provide a heavy and in-depth curriculum, but teachers can adapt the program for time and level.

You feel the standards handcuff you? There's enough in the Choices curriculum to hit the standards, while also leading your students to being experts on a topic. Do you feel the standards limit your ability to take time to really dive into content? No matter. Choices is organized in such a way that teachers can use a day's worth of it or spend a week on a lesson. Choices is adaptable, like good teachers and students.

Get Them Moving

Once students feel like experts in a topic, it's time to add some action. Granted, students have already played an active role by researching the material on their own and discussing the material with their group partners, but how can we get them out of their seat?

Students can present their findings to their classmates in the classroom, but that can get stale after a while. Try inviting a panel of judges to your class. Or try holding an assembly where your students make their cases to the school (or to the entire sophomore class). Or, if the students worked on a human rights unit, maybe they organize a fair trade event. Or ask your students to create a public service announcement about the topic—respect for women in India, for example.

Send students out of the classroom. This might be scary at first. Who will they disrupt? What will they break? Who knows! Once they get into the rhythm of leaving the room, experiencing the excitement and change, they'll respect the independence. Our students are so conditioned to sit and stay that they don't know what to do when they stand. They associate standing with social time. We want to turn standing into an alternate learning time, but in order to do so, we must structure it in a way that is engaging and meaningful.

Give the students an assignment of developing an information campaign. They come up with the signage and catchy messages, and then they go around the school for a period, posting their creative messages. Perhaps you've organized it with some other Social Studies teachers where your students walk into their room to push their campaign of knowledge.

We learn best (adults and kids) when moving around, engaging with what we're studying. John Medina, a developmental molecular biologist (whatever that is, sounds cool though), writes in his book *Brain Rules* about the importance physical activity has on the brain and memory. He also talks about the importance of naps (and boy, I'm totally in support of that one).

LET THEM BE INDEPENDENT

Now put it altogether. Give students the jumpstart with the necessary readings, films, websites, and all to become the expert. While they're doing that, find ways where they can move about, whether it's during their research, or as a means of assessment, or as a project. Once the students have gone this far, it's time for them to make their own choice.

Let the students decide where they want to go next with the topic. If they were researching human rights, now it's time for them to focus on a particular piece of the puzzle. Maybe one student wants to look further into human trafficking, another wants to study child soldiers, another wants to look at police brutality, another wants to look at crimes against journalists, and another wants to examine the rights of musical artists and their online material. There's a zillion options out there.

While the class is covering the usual World History content, students are working on their own interest on the side. From time to time, students update the class on where they are on their research or interesting discoveries.

The students made the choice to study their topic. They, and only they, are the expert on their topic. They are enlightening the teacher and the rest of the class. This is a powerful motivator.

And who cares what the topic is? Who cares if it's not specified by the state standards? The point is that students are practicing critical-thinking skills. They are practicing presentation skills. And they did it all while reading about something they were interested in learning about. And by the way, you can finagle just about anything to fit the standards, so long as you're doing it for the students.

As Social Studies teachers, we want students to get involved in their community and their education. We want the experience to be real and valuable for them. We want them to take the skills they learn in our classes to their next class, or even better, to college and their future career.

There isn't much room for memorization of dates and dead people, but there is plenty of room for Social Studies. So, let's buck the current system.

CLOSING THOUGHT

In November 2015, the Obama administration announced its funding for Next Generation high schools. As the White House website puts it, the goal is to support "more personalized and active learning" and "access to real-world and hands-on learning."

We need to take hold of this and define just what Next Generation means. It's just the legitimacy we need to direct the education industry on the right path, but we need to convince the government of the importance of the Humanities. It's great to place students in real-life decision-making situations, but we can't forget to place it into a human context, one that builds moral character.

NOTE

1. The Era of Absolutism, Richelieu, and Louis XIV, and all that jazz, is one of my favorites. I loved the *Three Musketeers* growing up, and I love touring the sites across Europe, including Louis's Versailles and St. Martin's Cathedral in Bratislava, where my fave monarch, Maria Theresa, was coronated.

Chapter Three

Depth over Breadth

Why do the standards for high school World History courses cover the European Renaissance to today with an emphasis on the West? One answer could be because it continues the junior high school content that left off with the Renaissance. Another answer could be, "because we want our children to have an awareness about the world beyond the United States," and another explanation could be, "Well, because that's just how it's been done for many, many years."

It's not so much that a history of the world course that uses Western civilization as its focus is bad—it's just that there's so much more history to explore. As stated in chapter 2, the fact that states mandate that students learn a specific version of world history is short-sighted and, quite honestly, lazy. Those writing the curriculum grew up on a certain history, so that's the history they push.

There are those late-night shows that take the camera to the streets to ask random passers-by history questions. Then the audience laughs or gasps when the random passer-by doesn't know the answer—and probably at that moment some legislator somewhere has already begun writing a new piece of content to mandate into the state education standards. The legislator is thinking, "That kid didn't know the 16th Amendment! Here's my chance to make a name for myself! First step? Find out what the 16th Amendment says."

Let's take a step back. Maybe the interviewer is asking a veterinarian about who the United States fought in the Spanish-American War, and the veterinarian blanked on camera and said, "Germany?" But if that veterinarian asked the interviewer how to address the broken leg of an iguana, the interviewer would probably blank and say, "Germany?"

Does it matter if someone knows who fought in what war? And if someone knows every country that fought in every war ever, is that beneficial to anyone in any way? Heck, the veterinarian could have just pulled out her phone and found the answer online in ten seconds if she wanted, as could anyone today.

What basic memorization fact can't be found with a quick search on the phone?

The traditional history course is built from a belief that certain facts in history must be memorized. But what facts are most important to memorize? Most people don't know most history facts, but that doesn't mean they can't be successful in their field. In fact, they're probably successful in their field *because* they didn't bother memorizing history facts and instead spent time putting their brain to use.

DEPTH OF STORIES

Breadth won't capture the imagination. We're setting our students up for failure and boredom by requiring them to follow us on a tour of history lite, a sort of watered-down version that is easy to consume but that leaves a bitter aftertaste.

When we promote almost history as history, we twist and, quite honestly disrespect, history.

Students drop their head, defeated, claiming, "I'm just not good at history," and the reality is that they're not good at memorizing—not history.

Zenith Irfan was a twenty-one-year-old Pakistani woman who decided to live out her father's legacy and ride across her country. She had never gone much farther than her hometown outside of the studies she would have followed in school. She never knew the beauty of her own country before she took the leap to experience the "shock of beauty."

As Zenith spoke to Public Radio International's Marco Werman of *The World* in February 2016, she spoke of the amazing physical and spiritual experience of her travels on the motorcycle.

Werman directed Zenith to her own Facebook page where she quotes the Prophet Muhammad, "Don't tell me how much educated you are, tell me how much you traveled."

Zenith explains herself by referring to school and how students are always asked to learn concepts and definitions but rarely asked to *experience them.* Zenith goes on to give appreciation and respect to learning from books, but she stresses the importance of experiencing and how that develops the mind and *whole spiritual being.*

Zenith's experiment is an extreme, no doubt. There are probably few courses that ride students across the country—but, heck, what a course! Someone develop that one now!

Zenith's story illustrates the power of experiential learning and depth over breadth. She wasn't taking a whiff of a scratch-and-sniff sticker of a deep-fried candy bar. Nope. She was taking that deep-fried candy bar, spraying it with whipped cream, and chewing each bite thirty times to ensure maximum taste bud explosion.

DEPTH OVER BREADTH

Let's look at two cases of depth over breadth:

1. Drive a few dozen miles from Akron, Ohio, and you'll find yourself in Amish country. One Amish gentleman was asked by a school to build a prototype standing desk for a high school classroom. With nothing more than his mind and experience, he rattled off numbers and possible solutions and necessities that a high school desk had to have in order to endure the constant adolescent abuse.

   His shop looks antiquated but is pristine. His son follows suit in the mastery of this art—all on an eighth-grade education. There were no instructions to follow for building the desk. There wasn't a textbook with the chapter, "Building a Standing Desk." How did the son learn how to build without a textbook or a high school education? He lived it.

2. Let's go across the Atlantic. Take a glance at Germany's apprenticeship system. The United States currently looks at the German manufacturing sector in awe. How do those Germans manage such manufacturing? Students learn the textbook stuff in class, and then it is reinforced by time working in the trade. Can this model be adopted in the United States? Can it be adapted to fit service jobs in addition to manufacturing?

Both depth over breadth examples produce highly skilled and successful people who contribute to society and create a sustainable economy. There's no shame in them just because they are different from what we are used to.

Consider the Platt Technical High School in Milford, Connecticut. Such non-traditional schools provide students with skills sought after by computer giants like IBM. In a *U.S. News and World Report* article from December 2015, Randi Weingarten and Stanley Litow wrote, "Career and technical education, properly delivered, can provide a powerful link between school, college and career." Their article goes on to say, "It can motivate students through hands-on, project-based learning connected to interesting industries and careers."

REVOLUTIONARY CREATIVITY

There are students who love history, gobble it up, want more, and these students could be best served by creating apprenticeship-type experiences for them while in high school.

U.S. History teacher Jason Anderson of Archbishop Hoban High School in Akron, Ohio, does just this with his Revolutionary War program.

Each year, Jason organizes (with the blessing of Mount Vernon) a Revolutionary War Day. He and his senior student helpers erect their version of Fort Laurens (Ohio's only Revolutionary War fort) on the grounds of the school. The fort is complete with an officer's quarters, printing press station, a commissary serving coffee heated over a fire pit dug and maintained by students, surveying equipment, a field to play colonial games, a medical tent with tools you'd never want to believe were used for operating on humans, a collection of muskets (not real, but boy, do they look the part), and some other pretty great eye-catching stations.

During the event, Anderson's students (dressed in vintage uniforms, dresses, and other throwback visuals) lead visiting fifth grade students from station to station, where the fifth graders from the area experience life as an enlisted soldier in General Washington's army.

Not only do the high school students run the show at their own school, but Anderson takes the experience on the road to other schools in Ohio and even to Washington's Mount Vernon home.

Each year, Anderson has expanded the experience for students. Now, in order for students to qualify to take part in leading the Revolutionary War Day, students must work on an independent study, where they work with the Special Collections of the Akron's Main Branch Library (led by the wonderfully helpful Judy James), looking over grave records in order to learn about Revolutionary War veterans who are buried in the area. Through those records, students are able to learn a lot about the men and women they are portraying during the big event. Add the ease of filing through genealogy records, and the students come away with a strong understanding of whomever it is they have chosen to embody on Revolutionary War Day.

This is not a typical class, and that's what allows the students to go beyond the usual, but how did this happen? Because a teacher wanted to give his students the experience. And this is all done as an extension of the regular U.S. History class—a sort of apprenticeship.

REBOOTING PERSONALITY

The Revolutionary War event is associated with the U.S. History course, but it is entirely separate creation—it can stand alone. Teachers do not have to create an entirely new event to help build depth. In fact, we should start with the current courses we have before we decide to build new ones. So, what are some ways to give our current courses some personality? Let's use a World History course as our example.

1. **The 1800s through the steam engine.** The 1800s in a common World History course is always so difficult: nationalism, industry, imperialism—interconnected pieces, all important, but such a deep topic by themselves, there's very little room for all them in a course, and history teachers try to fit them all in. The usual World History course doesn't really allot much time for these three topics—spend a week on each and get to World War I. So, we could either build a semester course on 1800s Europe, or we could split the class into three topics, and that's what those students study for the next three weeks. In fact, give each student in those smaller groups one topic to become the expert on—the steam engine for instance.

    Side Note: We teach a history that jumps from one war to the next. Is there another way to string the years together? We teach about war over and over to the point of war being the focus. Thus, war becomes quite common, the norm. If we are to use wars as the focus of our history courses, we should ask ourselves, "What's the point?" Is it the war that's the important focus, or is it the case of the war and the effect that will best serve our students?

2. **Imperialism.** Imperialism is an interesting one because we often look at it through the lens of the place that does the dominating, and rarely do we look at it through the lens of the country that's being played. It's hard, because us Westerners aren't accustomed to it, but spend a week with your class, examining "the other places." Consider assigning different parts of the world to different groups: Kongo, Moghul Empire, the Ming Dynasty, the Inca. Do this first together with Cortes and the Aztecs. Look at art from both sides—how did they view each other? Look at Cortes's letters back to the monarchy. Present students with information on the Aztecs before the conquistadors arrived. What do we know about these people whose way of life and culture would be obliterated?

3. *Gunga Din.* Let me preface this by saying, if there's anyone out there who's game for making blockbusterish films, minus the blood and swearing, that address themes that can be used in our history classes, I'm in! Please do it! In the meantime, here's a suggestion: *Gunga Din.* This movie, as so many Hollywood films do, includes evidence of imperialism, but it also unapologetically includes orientalism, or *the other*, or the White Man's Burden. The 1939 gem *Gunga Din* is perfect for this. Just ask your students to "embrace the cheese."

Ask your students to watch the film through the perspective of the 1930s or Hollywood's perspective. Who are the actors who portray the characters? For instance, in *Gunga Din*, why does a Jewish actor born in New York City (Sam Jaffe) play Gunga Din? Why does an Italian actor play the evil Thuggee leader? Why can three British soldiers easily battle dozens of Indians? Who wrote *Gunga Din*? So many good investigative and thought-provoking questions can come from a single film. Similar questions can be pondered during the watching of *The Man Who Would Be King* or *The Quiet American*.

DEBUGGING BRAINS

Debug those brains! In fact, using pop culture is a good tool for debugging children's brains.

There's a lot out there that streams into the kid brain without a filter. Unfiltered information can lead to negative consequences. Students might be left believing watered-down versions of history. Students might attach themselves to biased viewpoints of history. Students might just hear something wrong and come to view it as fact.

It's no secret that we are mostly shown movies and television and pictures and advertisements and whatever else that lacks "worldliness," and this thus leads to a rather myopic view of the world. Such a single-minded perspective doesn't challenge the brain. If anything, it stunts the growth of the brain. It's like bench-pressing fifty pounds for your entire life.

There should be a course called Debugging the Brains, where you challenge all that the students have come to believe as fact, or you call on students to dig deeper into concepts that have been dumbed down. Take the Nazi's Aryan race idea. What did it really mean? Where did the Nazis get the idea? Did they really only like blonde people? If so, what about the hair color of most every Nazi leader?

Debug those brains!

Teachers can write lessons about the Holocaust. Teachers can make it engaging by having the students investigate websites that elaborate on the buildings at Auschwitz. Teachers can take a field trip to the Maltz Museum of Jewish Heritage. Teachers can bring in a speaker, giving students a lot to think about for a reflective piece to be presented in class.

Teachers can later discuss the Nuremberg Trials, but it's not long before the world history class is off into the Cold War, examining the proxy wars between the United States and the Soviets.

A course that focuses on human rights solely does not only provide a common theme for the students, but it also allows time for the students to really grapple with the concepts of genocide or the Geneva Conventions. Students thus have the depth of understanding to feel confident offering their perspectives and supporting those perspectives with a variety of sources.

We dabble in this now, providing a week or two for students to work through units before we're off to the next one, which doesn't give the students much time to make sense of the units, or for that matter, care about the subject matter. "What do I need to know for the test?"

But if we construct courses that are focused on one topic, that carry a single theme, that can engage with the historic subject, that give students the time to ponder a question over a long period of time, that allows students to become experts on a topic, then we've created a course that helps students strengthen their critical-thinking skills.

A final suggestion on implementing a more focused, in-depth lesson: reality-based learning and role-playing. Let's use the rebel printers of the seventeenth century for our example.

Following the introduction of moveable print into Europe, monarchs soon realized they had a new enemy: rebel printers. Kings and queens rushed to charter their own publishers—the only legal publishers—controlling the words that their subjects would read. However, it didn't take long for underground printers to begin secretly spreading their pamphlets. Ask your students to take on the role of the rebel printers.

What if the class is divided into teams of rebel printers, each with its own agenda, each responsible for educating the subjects of the monarchy about a particular key idea?

Build in an extra layer of fun, where the rebel printers relate the topics, such as debates over the Protestant Reformation, to the school, and you as the monarchical teacher or the principal.

Ask the students to go deeper yet. The printers could include the most recent celebrity news and scandals, given the intrigue of Europe's royal families. Students could examine the attempts by monarchs to censor the press, such as the Star Chamber Decree of 1637. Teachers could further the learning experience by asking students to deliberate over historic and modern examples of freedom of speech.

The point of the rebel printer's idea is for students to play the role, to extend themselves to the lives of printers of the seventeenth century, for students to find a sense of empathy. Through the lens of that one rebel printer, students could examine many realities and debates of the 1600s.

A great course would be one that examined one caravan's adventure along the Silk Road. Start with something familiar to the students, such as Rome, and follow the traders on their adventure, venturing first to Alexandria, then on to Tyre, through the Fertile Crescent along the Tigris, toward the Persian world, into Buddhist and Hindu regions, and into the world controlled by the Han Dynasty. In each region, the students recreate the cities and culture.

CLOSING THOUGHT

If the goal is to build a more focused, in-depth curriculum, then teachers will have to have a strong understanding of the material. Enter the need for professional development workshops and courses. For example, if your students are spending time researching the impacts of the Holocaust, then perhaps it's time you check out the International Committee of the Red Cross Exploring Humanitarian Law resources or workshops. EHL provides materials that help teachers and students gain background knowledge on International Humanitarian Law, before being asked to put the laws into action. Together, you and your students will analyze scenarios that assist you in discussing questions, such as "What should a soldier do on the battlefield when confronted with a wounded combatant?"

Chapter Four

Deconstructing the Doldrums

HIGH SCHOOL WORLD HISTORY COURSES ARE THE WORST

Consider how this sounds to students: "Class, our next unit of study is the Age of Science, where we're talking about how an Italian guy looks through a telescope to see the rings of Saturn!" Slouched kids respond by covertly checking their phones to see who just texted them. And who can blame them?

Just a week prior to this statement, the students read in their textbooks about the frescoes of Michelangelo, and prior to that, they worked together in examining the effects of the Black Plague, and in between, they probably didn't learn about Jan Hus. As the students look ahead, they can see that they'll next learn about how the compass aided the Age of Discovery, where Spanish people slaughter other people, who usually don't have names.

Trying to wrap one's head around all of these topics seems daunting, especially if the goal is to teach, well . . . teach what?

In U.S. History classes (or American History as it is called in Ohio), we demand our students learn about George Washington and Thomas Jefferson, and we shake our heads at people who can't recall information about these two historical characters.

We hear a lot about our Founding Fathers. Our Founding Fathers did this. Our Founding Fathers did that. The point is, they *did* do things. They didn't memorize.

If our Founding Fathers had only memorized facts about the Enlightenment, would they have been able to apply their knowledge? Would they have acted on their belief about the concept of rights? Or would they have just known that rights exist? Would they have sat, drinking their rum, challenging each other to recite the pages of John Locke's *Two Treatises*?

Whether it's the massive amount of content in a World History course or the memorization of a U.S. History course, there's something missing.

Here's the point: What do we want the students to know? What is the point? We can pout about kids not getting it, but we can also reflect on our own system to see why kids might not get it.

JAZZING UP THE DRAB

It's difficult to reimagine what high school could look like. The system has been in place for so long, that the structure of high school seems to have been part of the covenant made by Abraham with the All Mighty.

But let's not get down on ourselves. Rather than pout about the drab course that is World History, let's develop some ways that could spice up the course and speak to the students, building something more relevant. How can teachers work with the current clunky course they have and build new ideas from within?

What can teachers do in their World History classes that deconstruct the doldrums, while still fulfilling the mandated content?

Consider a semester-long project that complements the content but extends it, and extends the content in such a way so that students can focus their attention and dig deep. But the project must be more than just research. The students have to put their findings into action. It must be something relevant. It must be something current—something not so distant, where the students feel connected. And it must be something where the students turn it into something real—not notes, not a multiple-choice test, not a PowerPoint presentation—something practical that uses skills that are needed for an innovative, creative, collaborative workplace.

The usual high school World History course covers the European Renaissance to today, or at least through the Cold War. One challenge for teachers is how to introduce non-Western topics to students in a World History course.

WORK WITH WHAT YA GOT

In his article *The Problem with High School Nostalgia*, Peter Cohen warns us about using our own high school memories to guide the future of education. He states that the curriculum must draw "connections to what students will one day do to earn a living."

Consider a project that extends the content—a sort of *side project*—where students work with partners on a topic of their choice over several months. Think of it as a kind of timeout from the usual content.

The project would focus on critical-thinking and problem-solving skills—still in line with the standards or Common Core, if you're into that sort of thing.

For example, during a World History class's discussion of the protectorates of France and Britain in the Middle East following World War I, consider extending the content on the Middle East—no doubt a subject high school students have heard about. The teacher could use current event days to address the most recent news of the Middle East, but why not make a project out of it? Build a project where students take the lead.

Consider a project on the water shortage in the Middle East or the destruction of historical places by ISIS or the current refugee crisis. Looking for a positive message? How about the number of female graduates from Tehran University outnumbering male graduates?

For the purposes of this chapter, let's settle on an example that examines the fleeing of people from the instability of Syria.

First, what is it we want our students to get out of this? What can students gain from studying the refugee crisis, and what content can be related back to the mandated course content?

Let's break it down:

1. **The basics:** Teachers provide sources for students so that students can gather the basics. What is a refugee? Who are the refugees in this case? Where are they going, and why are they going there? Here teachers could help students understand the basics, touching upon ethical decision-making, and allowing students to voice their beliefs and positions. Try *Frontline*'s "Children of Syria" video.
2. **Impacts:** What impacts are the people who are fleeing having on neighboring countries? Here, more technical subjects could be discussed. What is the economic impact on a country like Lebanon, which has taken in many fleeing Syrians, despite its own economic struggles? Students could examine the differing positions on whether or not to take more refugees into a country. Teachers could provide contrasting perspective pieces.
3. **Extend the lesson:** Understanding the situation and the in-depth examination of the situation is one thing, but how can teachers put all of this into action. For this, students will have to go a step further into the story. Where are these people going? Refugee camps. Ask students to examine different refugee camps and what exactly goes into a refugee camp: Do people work? Do kids play? Where do people pray? How do they get their water? Where does the food come from? A refugee camp in Jordan has its own soccer league—a positive story that's worth enjoying with the students.

4. **Application, part 1:** Once students have an understanding of the complicated and extensive workings of a refugee camp, ask students to build one of their own, being sure to remain true to costs, necessities, and employment, while including some glimmers of hope for the refugees to save both the hearts and minds of the people. Some refugee camps have more facilities than others, so be sure to introduce the students to a variety. In teams, students can begin building camps, being sure to reference articles that support why they have chosen to build what they have included in their camp. There's plenty that can be found online regarding designing refugee camps. There's camps that are misery, and there's camps with the newest innovations.

5. **Application, part 2:** Once the students have collaborated in agreeing on what they want their refugee camp to look like and why, then it's time for them to actually build the camp. Of course, teachers could ask their students to build a poster board that diagrams their camp, but does a teacher want thirty poster boards cluttering their room for the remainder of the school year? Consider allowing the students to choose for themselves how they want to display their created refugee camp.

6. **Application, twenty-first century:** Suggest to students that they build a virtual refugee camp (if they have the capabilities). There are plenty of games or apps that kids can get creative with in building their own worlds—in this case, a refugee camp. Students can freely build a refugee camp in Minecraft, or other similar building games, constructing grounds for the livestock, medical quarters, water sanitation, commissary, shelters, playground, makeshift cafe, grocery store, security, and so on. The list goes on and on, depending upon the difficulty level the teacher wants to set.

7. **Presentation:** Once students have studied and constructed their refugee camp, it's time for them to present their camp and why they built what they built, and why they put the sanitation where they put it, and what the shelters are made out of, and all the rest. Students have to support their decisions by referencing articles or studies that support their points. For instance, if a team of students build a rollercoaster[1] for the children in their Minecraft refugee camp, the students won't be able to support their argument with any valid source.

8. **Feedback:** Following a team's presentation, allow the students in the audience to give some constructive feedback or ask questions for clarification. Teachers could also allow students to try to find faults in their classmates' refugee camps. Students tend to enjoy finding holes in their colleagues' work. Deliberation is a great way to extend the understanding, as students construct respectful arguments and rebuttals.

A project such as the refugee camp project doesn't detract from the regular content of the course; it only enhances it and helps students strengthen their application skills. In addition, the project will allow for classroom time to discuss a topic familiar to the students, making it relevant in application and reality.

The focused and in-depth projects allow students to spend time on a topic for a long enough time to really examine the details, dissecting it so that students can see how complicated real life and real life decisions are.

Students will not be able to turn to the student go-to response of "just blow 'em up" or "just divide it equally" because they won't find any valid evidence to support such claims. Such concentrated inquiry also allows for students to become experts. Students are much more likely to take ownership and participate when they feel like an expert on a topic. They've done the research. They've discussed it with their group members. They've made the decision on what to extract from the readings. On the other hand, when students feel inadequate or distant from a topic, they can't take ownership, they won't feel a connection, and, as a result, they won't act.

A mere studying of or reading about refugees not only lacks student engagement but it also fails to engage emotions. Our students, as well as most everybody reading this book, cannot comprehend the horrors people fleeing warfare face. However, by asking students to dig deep into the subject over a period of time, teachers lead their students to at least stepping in the direction of empathy.

Turning refugees into a multiple-choice question robs students from strengthening the development of their hearts and minds, and it also robs the refugees of a human face.

Education reforms move slowly, but teachers can enhance what they can now. We can't wait for an all-out revolutionary upheaval that transforms education for us.

QUICK SUGGESTIONS TO REBOOT THE USUAL

Let's take a moment to review the usual units in a ninth or tenth grade World History course. Included are quick suggestions for making each unit real.

1. **Renaissance:** First, to start a course with a Renaissance (rebirth) is an interesting choice. What is it a rebirth of? Anyway, let's reboot this unit by using the rebel printers idea from chapter 3.
2. **Scientific Revolution.** Let's reboot this unit by choosing one scientific achievement—one that can guide toward another topic. How about the compass? This brilliance can take us across the sea, explain the

power of Portugal and Spain around the globe, and drop us in the Americas for our next unit.

3. **Enlightenment:** Following an introduction to Locke and Rousseau and Montesquieu and Wollstonecraft, introduce students to modern debates regarding rights. Allow students to choose their own, like human or animal rights. But how about if we get a little more specific and relevant to the students' interests? How about the question whether or not college athletes should be paid?

4. **Revolutions:** Pull the students in by showing how enlightened thinking of the seventeenth and eighteenth centuries was explosive. Enter, the Arab Spring. Compare the French Revolution to the Syrian Civil War to demonstrate struggles in liberation and differences of opinion as to the direction of a revolution. War isn't always a simple one side versus another. Sometimes, war is one side versus one side versus one side versus . . . you get the idea.

5. **Imperialism:** There are zillions of stories that illustrate those in power taking advantage of the vulnerable. There are cartoons, books, movies. Use *Star Wars*, *The Lorax*, sports teams, *The Hunger Games*, *SpongeBob the Movie*, *Chronicles of Narnia*. Any one of these can be used to explain imperialism. If you want to get more serious, you could use Puerto Rico as a case study.

6. **Industry:** As the eras become more modern, it becomes easier to bring your own community into the storyline. In Akron, Ohio, the former strength of the tire industry can be used, but there was also a vibrant toy industry that might be more interesting and fun for students. A comparison to the modern toy industry could then be examined, looking at working conditions, as well as consumerism and advertisements.

7. **World War I:** History classes get pretty carried away with war. The units jump from war to war. This gets a little tiresome. The causes and impacts of the war are more important than the war itself. World War I usually starts with the Serbian ultra-nationalists, the Black Hand assassinating the Archduke of Austria-Hungary, but then both countries kind of disappear in the story and don't really return. Kind of anticlimactic. Instead, try sticking with Serbia and Austria. The two have some of the most drastic changes in territory. Serbia balloons into Yugoslavia and the Austrian Empire is left a tiny German state excluded from the rest of its German brothers and sisters. Ask students to examine this. Was this a just end to the war?

8. **Totalitarianism:** Try the totalitarian horror project. There are still plenty of authoritarian regimes around the world to examine. Or ask the students to act as an authoritarian regime to transform the school into a totalitarian system. Sure, some students will think the school is

already ruled by a dictator, but that's all the more reason to ask them to argue their point. Groups of students can build propaganda campaigns to show how they would hold on to power.

9. **World War II:** Outside of the Holocaust, there's very little concentration on the magnitude of destruction and horror caused by this war. Instead, we glamorize World War II as America's great triumph, and we patriotically hold it up as proof of our unlimited power. Still today, students use World War II to explain how the United States can't lose wars. Still, seventy years later. World War II is turning into a mythology, like Lincoln or Washington. Such myths don't build critical-thinking skills. World War II (and its sister World War I) are good conversation pieces to engage in discussions about why Europeans want to hold onto the European Union, and perhaps why some younger Europeans could care less about the EU.

10. **Cold War:** In a World History course, the bulk of the concentration in the Cold War unit is focused on the superpowers. There are a couple other directions teachers can go to bring some life to this. Try focusing on propaganda and the life in each country. There are plenty of Soviet ads on YouTube that provide a glimpse into the communist world. The investigative work researching life in the Soviet Union might lead to some interesting results. Another route is to focus on the proxy wars, from C.I.A.-led coups to the Soviet invasion of Afghanistan, the latter providing a great link from the Cold War to the modern struggle with Islamic extremism, as fighters in Afghanistan went back to their homes in their own countries following the war to spread anti-imperialist sentiments. The Cold War is useful in explaining why anti-Western views exist.

11. **Modern Age:** It would be quite revealing for the students to interview their parents or grandparents about life as a teenager and compare it to the students' life. For instance, how have choices in the grocery store or family time changed over time? And which is better—then or now? *Why do this?* Because it acts as an opportunity for students to gain firsthand accounts of events, practice interview skills, feel like an expert on a topic when sharing with the class, and maybe is the beginning of taking a step further into studying a topic.

Finally, for each of these units, consider taking a look at it from an angle you never have done before in class. Look at the Austrian frontlines during World War I. Examine totalitarianism through the story of the fourteen families in El Salvador. Focus on the United States in China during World War II and the relationship with Chiang Kai-shek. Talk about complicated, study the Angolan civil war when discussing the roles of the superpowers during the

Cold War. Or check out the popular milk bars in Poland during the rule of communism.

Themes

And now for an all-out reconfiguration of a World History course. The standards are a little confining when it comes to a complete restructuring of a World History course, but there are some options. Let's try one option on for size.

It's understood there is certain content that is mandated that all students learn. In the Social Studies, this is dictated by the standards. One way to expand the options is to challenge the students with an independent study, which will be discussed in chapter 6. Independent studies use and strengthen problem-solving skills, while asking student to look at the mandated content differently.

Try a thematic approach—something as specific as *human rights* or something as vague as *power* or *changes in power*. Or include an ethical theme by asking the students to keep a morals log, where they determine the moral impact of people or events.

Let's again use the traditional textbook units, but this time, let's experiment with how human rights and social justice can be applied.

1. **Renaissance.** What rights did exist for the Italian republics, like Florence? How did people vote, and were they tried in court fairly? Was there a difference for men and women? What control did some families like the Medici have, and is there anything like that today? Were people free to be an individual, or was societal norms too constraining. "Don't be born a woman if you want your own way," wrote Nannina de Medici.
2. **Scientific Revolution**. Examine Galileo's fate through the hands of human rights. Was he free to practice science? How did the Inquisition deal with him? Fairly? What constitutes fair? Were Galileo's rights compromised because of other forces?
3. **Enlightenment**. This one is basically built on a fight for human rights, but let's twist it up and look at the Irish and the English during the Enlightenment. How did one group abuse the rights of another? Where were the Irish allowed to farm? Where could they fish?
4. **Revolutions**. There's not much on the peasants in France during the revolution, mainly because nobody cared much about them, and you weren't going to find an educated peasant, but who lost more heads during this revolution? Or, follow the story of Olympe de Gouges and her head.

5. **Imperialism**. Must I say any more? The majority of the Age of Imperialism includes events that fail to respect the rights of human beings.
   The carving up of Africa by a few guys in Berlin. Ask students to
   consider what happens when people who are unaware of the reality of
   a land and the people have the power to draw borders for that land and
   people. You could hand your students a map of their town and ask
   them to carve up their town into strict boundaries that can't be
   crossed. How would the people in those regions be affected? You
   could also select one specific story like Belgium's King Leopold and
   his genocide of the people of Congo.
6. **Industry**. How about looking at the Industrial Revolution and the
   cotton gin and the rush for more slave labor in the American South.
   The Lowell Mill girls of Massachusetts make for a good story too, if
   you want to talk human rights.
7. **World War I**. Extend this war's story into the militarization and the
   nationalism of Europe during the 1800s, both of which led to the
   Italian fight for unification. Following the battle of Solferino, the
   wounded lie suffering on the battlefield. The carnage moved Jean
   Henri-Dunant, leading eventually to the Geneva Conventions and the
   International Committee of the Red Cross. The devastation left by
   World War I would further support a push for the rights of non-
   combatants.
8. **Totalitarianism**. Following World War I, there were many people
   around the globe who thought they might become free, given Woo-
   drow Wilson's point of self-determination. In 1919, protests and re-
   volts and rallies erupted all over the world. The Korean people, for
   instance, thought they would gain their freedom from the Japanese.
   This, however, would not happen.
9. **World War II**. This unit is essentially based in the complete destruction of human rights, and examining the efforts after the war to solidify rights is essential for students. Following the war, the International
   Declaration of Human Rights were designed to ensure nothing like the
   Holocaust could happen again. The United Nations, similarly, is established at this time, and Eleanor Roosevelt represented the United
   States. Another topic that makes for a good debate is the Nuremberg
   Trials. The aim was to establish a fair trial, but could these men, given
   the world emotions, have a fair trial?
10. **Cold War**. The U.S. civil rights movement might not be considered a
    world affair, but the Russians sure used it to their advantage, pointing
    to it as an example of U.S. racism. Not to mention, the United States
    supported South Africa. How can a country's lack of human rights act
    as an opportunity for an enemy?

Take any one of the ideas in this chapter and use it to enhance an already existing unit. Or, heck, use it in place of a current unit. Set aside your textbook and pick up one of the suggested ideas.

Begin distancing yourself from looking to your textbook first. Author of *Lies My Teacher Told Me*, Jim Loewen challenges the doldrums of the traditional textbook, how they gloss over facts, while omitting others. There's plenty that textbooks omit, partly because it's impossible to include everything, and partly because they want to, but purposeful omissions from history provide only half truths.

CLOSING THOUGHT

Deconstruct the doldrums of history. Don't take what currently exists for granted. Take it apart instead and reconstruct it in a way that benefits students' understanding of how the world works. Reconstruct history in a way that challenges students. Reconstruct it in a way that enhances students' problem-solving skills and creativity.

NOTE

1. From experience, let me just say that the Minecraft refugee camp rollercoaster a student constructed and showed in class was pretty amazing, but obviously isn't economically practical for a true camp. At the same time, I'd suggest to the students that they don't include a bunch of pigs in their Minecraft camp for food if the camp is situated in Lebanon or any other Muslim-dominated region.

Chapter Five

I Didn't Learn This in College

Now, for a letter from the author to young or aspiring teachers:

Dear Young or Aspiring Teacher,

I've been lucky to keep a lot of my youthful energy and positivity. Some of it is an innate, immature character trait, and some is learned. It's not always easy to hold on to the excitement of the first years of teaching. Distractions occur. Age accumulates. Administrative gobbledygook quickly attaches itself on teachers like unsightly barnacles, and if you're not careful, can lead you astray.

Over the course of a career, teachers attend dozens of workshops and conventions filled with education jargon, and teachers are encouraged to adopt the jargon.

Beware.

Before too long, the jargon can replace the purpose. You'll find yourself understanding and using words like "ascertain" and "coalesce." You'll quickly begin talking about how to "scaffold" or "differentiate." The words will come first, the students second.

I found it helpful, in order to stay on the same plane with the students, to avoid the attack of the words.

Naïveté often carries a negative connotation. On the contrary, it can be quite powerful and positive.

The naïveté doesn't have to bleed into your content. You can still be an expert in your International Politics class, understanding the callousness and Realpolitik of that world, but maintain a spark of positive youthfulness in the classroom. The students relate better to the naïveté. You'll also reduce the number of gray hairs.

Embrace the naïveté.

Sincerely,

Greg Milo

This is an important chapter. Firstly, it provides a sort of break in the action from the abundance of ideas being proposed to you. Secondly, it's good to know that the ideas being proposed might work sometimes and might not work other times, and for some of you, the ideas proposed might be way off the mark. And all that's fine.

Teachers are driven and motivated by the belief that they can inspire all students—the teachers just need to believe. However, there will be some students you won't connect with no matter your tactic, but that's okay.

There's no need to give up on a student just because you're not connecting. It might be that you're not connecting at that moment, but years down the road, a spark that you set in that student might go off and inspire her.

There will also be the days where you connect with none of your students. Sometimes you'll praise a student, and he'll react with no emotion, as if he is a wax creature. But that's just the way it is.

Sometimes you'll try to motivate your students by continually changing up your lessons, and the students will thank you with an over-exaggerated sigh. Sometimes you'll think back to your university course on instructional methods and assign jobs to your students so they feel invested and important, and the students will ask, "Is this for points?"

Sometimes you'll ask your students for feedback about the class, and instead, you receive zero suggestions, just sniffles and yawns.

None of the strategies work all the time.

You'll have moments where you believe you've developed the most perfect and clear instructions, and students will respond with, "I'm so confused."

You'll have moments where you think you've built the most creative and interactive lesson in the world and the students will instead use the time you've given them to gossip about the most recent Snapchat phenomenon.

Young teachers must be prepared for the obstacle course they will have to leap over and dive under to succeed. Veteran teachers must have the opportunity to vent and know that there are others battling for the same cause despite the resistance.

Whatever the case, it seems only right for a book on education to include a break, like a spring break, or at least some time to chill in the teacher lounge.

So, think of this chapter as a getaway for veteran teachers and some hints for young teachers.

NOT EVEN GREAT IDEAS ALWAYS WORK

Nothing in this book is full proof. And that's another thing to keep in mind. Trying—whether or not every detail is perfect—is the key. Don't wait for the perfect plan; you'll never get there. Don't be afraid to try your best and learn from your mistakes. Make the engaging projects your own, but you'll first have to try them out to see what works and what you like.

Theories are ideas thought of by other people who are not you. Think your own theories.

But don't give up on your theories right away. Keep working on them. If there's a subject or idea that really motivates you, run with it and turn it into something special for your students.

Not all great ideas work all the time.

Take some of these stories for example:

Say you plan a trip overseas that includes stops in Krakow, Prague, and Berlin. You've worked really hard, planning for months, making sure that every excursion and every stop and everything in between is perfect.

You themed the trip *Old and New*, a take on World War II and the Cold War, and the students worked hard and never complained, no matter how jam-packed the days were with activities. You're certain that everyone involved has gotten some deep meaning from the excursion, and you're certain that the students will have no problem building their experience into a creative project that demonstrates their new expertise.

It comes to the final evening, and you're enjoying a loving traditional Schwabisch dish in Berlin, out for dinner for your final meal. The group is discussing some of their favorite moments, and you find it exhilarating to hear the students talk quite articulately about specific moments—explanations of history and culture most people haven't a clue about.

One students references the John Lennon Wall in Prague. It's a graffitied wall dedicated to the imagination and peace efforts of Lennon—a magical place for a Beatles fan. During the Cold War, youth spray-painted the wall with words and images. The wall sat just beyond the French Embassy, and the rebellious youth knew that the authorities wouldn't risk any violent scenes outside the embassy walls, so away they spray-painted.

The student, excited to talk about one of her top moments says, "I liked the John Legend Wall."

"John Lennon, you mean?"

"Whatever."

And in that moment, it strikes you that the trip wasn't as perfect as you thought. Not every student understood the meaning of everything they encountered on the trip.

Hours of planning, mounds of work and responsibility, thousands of miles and dollars, and a student flushed it down the toilet with that one slip. Of course, it is just an innocent mix-up, that's okay.

The *John Legend Scenario* illustrates that no trip can be perfect, but you can always use those less-than-perfect moments as a chance to continue the conversation about the misunderstanding. A teachable moment, they say.

When planning elaborate projects for your students, you really just have to be courageous enough to endure some blunders.

PROJECT HOPE

Every Wednesday night for seven years, rain or snow shower, summer or winter break, Project HOPE led groups of students out to the streets of Akron to hang out with our less fortunate Akronite friends, men and women often swept under the concrete by the city.

Project HOPE developed into a popular activity for students, whether they used it for service hours or not. Students came back after having graduated to participate in Project HOPE and to see friends they had made.

The entire goal of Project HOPE was to present students with a different reality, to take them from their comfort zone, and to get them to actively engage with people. It was all about building human relationships and practicing that humanity.

Project HOPE was as raw as you could make a high school experience. Over the seven years, some of what the students encountered was ugly. Students talked with people struggling with chemical abuse and human abuse. Students saw people at their lowest, but the students brought a positivity that brightened many people's day.

Project HOPE never expected that they would be relied upon to bring weekly hope. Some people waited all week for the students to bring their smiles.

Some nights sat heavy on the soul. There's a certain something that happens inside when a barefoot kid walks up to the back of a van asking for food—gut-wrenching.

The team of HOPE'sters talk each night about what they encountered, who they talked with, and what they felt. The idea was to get students to reflect deeply. The leading teachers didn't want to hear, "I liked it." Instead, the teachers wanted names and specifics and the students to use their words to articulate their feelings.

For the most part, the students surprised teachers. If teachers wanted, they could sit in the van while the students talked and listened with their friends.

Student reflections were great, and often there were reflections that made the teachers stop and think.

However, the teachers' intentions didn't always pan out. There were times, though few, where students just didn't get it.

It was a chilled and rainy evening. The team of Project HOPE had attempted to reach out to a new population they had caught wind of. The HOPE'sters parked on the edge of a wooded area and searched around for some tents for a bit. The team saw trails but no people. Just as they were about to take off, a man appeared from the woods. He stopped short of walking completely from the woods. A student called out to him, but he seemed uninterested in the food or fellowship. He just stared and walked away.

That night, when Project HOPE returned back from our adventure, the students offered up their thoughts. Students spoke of joyful conversations and unfortunate ones. They disclosed their worry for some of our friends and their happiness for others. And then, a student who hadn't offered up any reflective words spoke.

"I liked when the guy stared at us from the woods."

"Why?"

"It was funny."

The teachers pressed him for a little more depth but there was none, and afterwards, when all the students had left, the teachers agreed that Project HOPE hadn't quite reached everyone that night.

FOLLOWING DIRECTIONS

In the case of the "man in the woods," a single student didn't quite get it. But sometimes, there are majorities that don't get what you think is a great idea. You've planned for weeks, written the most creative lesson, and when it's put into practice, you witness a flop.

The project that comes to mind involved students practicing their interviewing skills. Ultimately, students would be interviewing community leaders about their specialty. Students would film the interviews, edit them if necessary, and post the videos on their websites.

The practice interview involved students talking with neighbors or grandparents or anyone not of their immediate family about how the city was different during their childhood.

The teacher talked about methods behind strong videos. Basically, she was looking for short, to-the-point interviews with close-cropped interviewees, nothing filmed from a distance. The teacher even said, based on experience, "Don't film anyone from a distance while they lounge on their couch."

The teacher brought into the classroom the public library's director of the Digital Media Center, someone who wrote a curriculum on citizen journalism. He gave students pointers on how to make a viewable video.

The teacher's ultimate hope was to encourage students to engage with others, hone communication skills, and work on website skills. In the end, they would present their work.

The day came for the students to show what they had posted on their websites. Interview after interview was of a parent sitting on a couch from a distance. A maddening buzz droned throughout the interview, probably a refrigerator or air conditioning.

The teacher was dumbfounded, completely at a loss. The only thing she could do was use the opportunity to her advantage.

"Basically, what you all showed today is exactly what your video should not look like," the teacher explained bluntly. "You've basically created the blueprint for what not to do."

The teacher wondered if her words came across too harshly, but for the remainder of the semester, the students' videos included no couches.

There's something difficult about attending a convention and successfully bringing the excitement back to the classroom.

It's always great to hear from other educators. Sometimes it gives you that newly charged spark that ignites inspiration. Here's one of those times where the enthusiasm of a convention turned maddening.

A Social Studies teacher was in Los Angeles, attending the ASCD Conference when he got the idea for what would eventually become a new course. And it was during the conference where he got the idea to use Minecraft for a project on refugee camps.

He sat, his mind racing to catch up with the emerging ideas in his head, half listening and half writing. The presenter spoke of making education real, giving students a voice, utilizing community resources.

The teacher wondered how he could get his students involved in the local community when he taught world history courses?

Then it hit him. He found an angle. One of the purposes of his World History course was to present students with different cultures. He figured he had a nearby culture to study: Akron, Ohio. Further, the teacher thought, if his job was to facilitate critical thinking, if his job was to work with students on their problem solving, if his job was to inspire action and initiative in students, then utilizing the hometown would be much more sensible than Revolutionary France.

The teacher scribbled notes as fast as he could. He designed a project called *This Is Akron*. The goal of the project was for students to define the city and build an event that commemorated the city for its bicentennial celebration in 2025. Students would research about the past and present and decide what they felt embodied the culture of the city. They would defend their decision and put their creativity to work by designing an event. Their final speech would be judged by a visitor from the community. The teacher jotted down some local experts he knew who would make great judges.

The teacher built a rubric, and built in benchmarks so he could check students' work. A lot of high-energy time was going into this idea that, when implemented, would surely motivate students and help them practice necessary skills. The teacher was pumped, and he couldn't wait to share his ideas with the faculty back home. He was going to be a teacher forever!

Upon his return, the teacher was immediately confronted with a problem with course numbers for his department following registration. This dilemma consumed his next week and soured his mood. It took less than a day for the energy from the conference to dissipate. More pressing administrative duties interfered.

One of the greatest difficulties is taking ideas and turning them into reality, especially when those ideas fuel your soul.

How do you take great ideas that inspire you and transform them into reality? How do you take your notes from an exciting conference in L.A. and do something with them before the usual school responsibilities begin draining your time and energy? Those are great ideas! Don't let them escape.

Enter, the Conference Buddy. Before you head to the convention, design a Google Doc that you fill in throughout the conference, or you could just simply keep a notebook. Either way, the Conference Buddy should be something you fill out immediately after the conference—maybe on the way home. It's something to help organize your thoughts.

Consider these possible categories for your Conference Buddy:

1. Quick thoughts on how to implement the idea. Don't worry about specifics here—just get the idea out.
2. What was inspirational and why? You might have to explain your excitement to someone in order to spread the excitement, so get ready.
3. Takeaways just for me.
4. Articles or books I heard about.
5. Methodologies I heard about. Differentiated instructions.
6. Big vs. small projects. What can you get done now? What's something you can work on for the future?
7. Who can you pull in and help make this idea a reality?
8. Timeframe for implementation, keeping in mind that not everything has to be done immediately.

It's important to let the ideas kind of percolate. Wait for the idea to mature. As much as you'll want to get an idea off the ground as soon as possible, sometimes it works best if you let it age, like a good wine.

CLOSING THOUGHT

Bottom line: be okay with not being perfect. Get ideas out. Experiment. Learn from others. Stay fueled. Don't let ideas die—put them on life support for a while if necessary. When you play around with education, you'll come up with your own ideas and theories—things that work best for you, your personality and your specific students. Don't just take everything you hear from others as testament. Ideas might work for them, but the same ideas might not work for you.

Chapter Six

Independent Studies

Once again, it helps to settle on a goal for your school's Social Studies curriculum. Is it to memorize history, or is it to challenge students' creative and critical thinking skills? How do you test? What do you test? How do you merge your methodology with accountability?

It's difficult to establish an independent studies program if the state curriculum is rigidly interpreted. If your school is only interested in making sure students know about Tecumseh's fate at the hands of the United States, then there's little room for an interested student to take time to research the strategies of the Shawnee leader—diving deep into the how, why, and the motivation behind Tecumseh's actions. It takes a little liberty to expand and enhance the learning experience using an independent study.

If you're comfortable with using the required content as a springboard to launch a course to the next level, then imagining independent study options for your students will be a breeze.

Every piece of material in a textbook can be elaborated—that's nothing new. Students can be asked to act as Tecumseh or William Henry Harrison and write about their perspectives on the struggle during the War of 1812. Students could role play or debate about who was correct, given information that they found. And those are some cool ideas. But can students be given a real-life comparison?

Let's continue with the Native American theme for a moment.

THE OTHER

Some students in the Union have access to Native populations. For instance, students in Arizona could complete some pretty awesome mission work in Tuba City with the Navajo.

But there are no reservations in Ohio. How can one get around such a roadblock?

One focus is to look at U.S.-Native relations, but that might be too limiting. Again, the point isn't so much the content but the method. Use the U.S.-Native relations as a platform to examine other cultural collisions that fit your community. For instance, across the United States, large refugee populations exist, often near an international institute or some organization with a goal of assisting newcomers to the States.

Ask students to research the local refugee populations. Ask the students to engage with these populations. If newcomers have opened a Nepali dumpling shop nearby, visit and enjoy some delicious food in the process.

Why are some refugees accepted more than others? Ask students to compile some "intel." This is where the independent study comes in. Have interested students take a semester to work with refugees, talk with refugees, and attend festivals and concerts where new immigrants are displaying their talents and culture.

Perhaps students will visit a Buddhist temple and sit with a couple of monks and have a conversation. Not only could the students inquire about the differences of culture, but students could make some deductions themselves based on the conversation. Maybe there are certain requirements for the interview that the monks demand.

It's no violent battle between the Shawnee and Ohio settlers, but just as cultures clashed in the nineteenth century, cultural differences between Nepalese people and the older, established population exist, be it negative or positive, and that depends on the perspective.

Students could take the "other" study a step further. For higher levels of high school, students could examine the impact of a large refugee population on a community. Does it drain on social welfare programs? Do new entrepreneurs bring money and excitement into the community? How could the community take advantage? What have other communities done? That right there is a great independent study, all from the original content of the War of 1812.

If the students get to know the people by name (taking steps beyond the generic reference of refugee), hear stories, taste food, listen to music, then the students could write an article for a local media outlet. Students could present about their findings at school to a panel—bring in a new Nepali friend to help present. Man! How awesome would that be?

THE BRANCH FOR ACTION AND ENGAGEMENT

Independent studies can work within the traditional education framework, but if a school really wanted to blow it out of the water, the school could give independent studies its own home. How about a department called the Branch for Action and Engagement, or BAE.

Such a branch of the high school could organize internships, network with the community, link interested students with experts in the community, organize travel abroad experiences, invite guest speakers, and work with students to complete tasks associated with their independent study.

If a group of students wanted to promote fair trade at the school, they could work with Fair Trade Campaigns to become a fair-trade-certified school. They could organize fair trade sales and fashion shows. They could work with the administration to bring fair trade foods to the campus.

BAE could also work with the students to run their own fair trade cafe at the school. There's a few high schools across the country with student-run coffee shops—the Next Gen Personal Finance blog shares a list.

A fair trade cafe would teach students moral business practices, marketing skills, organizational skills, people skills, financial literacy skills, and entrepreneurial skills.

First, the fair trade component would link the students' efforts to a global effort. Students could research about fair trade cooperatives, what the pros and cons are, support fair trade outreach and educational efforts, invite speakers who advocate for fair trade and have experienced land-grabbing, all while selling fair trade coffee, tea, and chocolate.

If there is a committed crew of students, it isn't difficult to acquire a fair trade status for the school. But what an achievement! Together, a team of students can say that they succeeded in getting a fair trade clause into the student handbook!

A student-run cafe takes a lot of work. Someone has to count and take care of the cash. Someone has to schedule workers. Someone has to promote the event. And, heck, someone has to make good coffee. All of these are transferable skills from high school to real life—more so than memorizing the events of the War of 1812.

But, if the students are interested in history, they could include specials on the historically significant days. Or they could hold competitions based in historical knowledge. "Two for one, if you can define Keynesian economics," the students could promote, as they learn about the Works Projects Administration, and how their venture mirrors those New Deal efforts.

The buy-in by the students, the ownership, the feeling of trust—these are all huge motivators that will engage the students, not to mention the real-life skills.

The promotional campaigns for a student-led cafe (posters, announcements, newsletters, videos, social media, slogans, jingles, etc.) are fun and educational—for the students running the show, the entire school, students, *and* teachers.

Such a venture would definitely capture the attention and interest of local media, making a great opportunity for the students to be recognized by the community, in addition great press for the school.

Need a ringer? Top it off with a trip to a farmers' cooperative in Nicaragua—bam!

Fair trade companies like Equal Exchange would happily assist with getting the cafe up and rolling.

SYNERGETIC EDUCATION

What is the goal of a worthwhile independent study? To give students the opportunity to build leadership, personal research, and community skills.

For an independent study, there's nothing like using the immediate community. One of the great things about being a Social Studies teacher is that we study society, and guess what, society is all around. We essentially can investigate anything as an independent study.

What if you live in a very rural area with access to little international connections? Don't limit yourself. Use what you have. Even if you feel there isn't an international presence in your community, there's still hope. Ask your students to poll the community about an international topic, let's say immigrants or U.S. soldiers overseas.

Themes work too. Students can still study local culture even if they're in a world cultures class. Why not? There are different cultures all around—that's one of the benefits of living in the United States.

But beyond culture, placing a question to the students, no matter if it's domestic or international focus, can be a great learning experience for kids.

Case Study Time! Akron Early College High School teacher Brad Scott wanted his students to take an active role in the community, and he also wanted them to feel like someone in the community was taking notice of their work (and voice).

Scott searched and searched and found the perfect tool for what he wanted to accomplish and what he wanted for his students.

Scott found the Mikva Challenge.

We always hear, "Don't reinvent the wheel." Well, some of us enjoy making the wheel our own way, but there are experts out there for most everything, so before you start building your own project, unit, or lesson, check to see if there's one that exists that you can use or build from.

The Mikva Challenge has the goal Scott wanted. It provides students with the tools needed for building a strong speech about a topic they are passionate about. It supports the teacher during his or her work with the students, and—arguably the best part—it showed the students how their voice matters and that they can take action.

With the help of Mikva, Scott walked his students through the steps of building an argument and articulating that argument. While the class worked on making a case for something they chose, they also worked on speaking and listening skills.

Mikva supported Scott as he taught his students how to speak with confidence. The students' first task was to recite the ABCs to the rest of the class. Silly, yes, but something all of the students could confidently present to their classmates, not to mention the exercise built an element of community.

The students chose whatever topic was important to them. Some students chose to make cases against discrimination. A student argued her case against dress codes, while another spoke about texting and driving. One Muslim student challenged the crowd's assumptions. A kid informed the crowd about the statistics behind racial profiling, and yet another shocked the audience about his life being fatherless.

Then, when the day came for the students to give their speeches, they were met with a filled auditorium.

Brad invited local experts to judge the presentations. In attendance were board of education members, city council people, a county executive, a former mayor, state representatives, and, of course, the senior class president. An absolute powerhouse of a panel.

Here's a visual of the event's awesomeness:

A student stood at the front of the room and railed against standardized tests. He referenced source after source to solidify his case against the mandated measurements. He spoke eloquently and convincingly. With every word, those in attendance were convinced.

"Standardized tests are an unnecessary time consumption," the tenth grader affirmed.

The room felt giddy with anti-standardization.

Man, this is education.

If a Social Studies teacher's job is to help students build the skills needed in becoming participating citizens, then a textbook is the worst partner. Building real-life skills, such as arguing a case to a panel of city leaders, seems a better answer.

The students wrote speeches about how to fix their community—something relevant to them. And people were listening!

The students who argued their cases attend the Akron Early College High School (AECHS). One after another, the kids impressed the audience who attentively sat in the lecture hall of The University of Akron.

It's one thing to be impressed with a high school student's work, but it's another thing for them to hold the attention of the crowd for an hour, and to wow them with articulate arguments about how their society could be improved.

Mikva Challenge was built with the goal of giving a voice to youth. Its mission states, "We believe that if youth voice is included in decision-making, then policy makers will make more informed decisions."

Scott said, "My goal was to show students that they were important and their opinion was important, and that if they want their community or city to be great, it is up to them to make it great. No one will do it for them."

Nor will a standardized test.

In *The Motivated Brain*, Gregory and Kaufeldt write about the importance of giving students a voice. "It is amazing how incorporating personal information and likes and dislikes into learning can engage students who would otherwise be disengaged." So true. Treat the students like investors, like they have stock in all of this education stuff.

During Project Soapbox, the students held the floor, charismatically and convincingly pitching their cause—true experts in their field.

Sure, they were sixteen years old, but their disposition was anything but adolescent.

Students are motivated when they're allowed to choose content that matters to them. Students are motivated when they feel like people are listening. And students are motivated when they feel a teacher believes in them to tackle challenging tasks. Scott showed his confidence in his students by inviting outsiders to listen and judge.

Nearly as impressive as the presenters were the attending students. Through finger snaps, the crowd could agree with points nicely served by the presenter or encourage nervous presenters to keep going. It was a perfect display of camaraderie and courtesy, as if the entire lecture hall was working together.

All too often, classroom debates turn raucous, a spotlight for the loudest and most aggressive. Mikva teaches the students civility, so deliberation is productive. It promotes finger snapping and "wild applause" when appropriate.

"We studied great speeches by watching videos or listening," Scott said. The classes learned about structure, appeals, rhetoric, and attention grabbers. "While studying, we snapped and cheered wildly. This got the class used to it before the first student gave a speech."

More so than studying about the Industrial Revolution or Age of Absolutism, real-life experiences teach students skills on being active citizens. It's easy for high school students to be apathetic when they feel disconnected from the democratic process. It's easy for students to be cynical about government when all they learn about it is how white-haired aristocrats founded the nation. But ask them to argue something they believe in and it will give them the energy to participate in the democracy.

If we want the youth to be our leaders, to lead their country forward, then education will have to train students on how to successfully take action in our community.

Former Akron Mayor, Jeff Fusco, who was in attendance during the students' speeches, said, "The students from AECHS impressed everyone at the 2016 Project Soapbox. They were very well organized, sharp in delivery and most importantly convincing in their arguments. I especially liked the fact that they closed with action items asking listeners to help advance their cause."

A TOUCH OF ENHANCEMENT

Was this an enormous effort by Scott? Well, yes and no. First, he took two weeks to implement the pieces of Mikva he wanted. He had full support from his principal, and he integrated the speeches into the civil rights movement unit. So, yes, it took effort, but it wasn't a complete abandonment of the U.S. History content he was required to teach. Rather, the speeches stressed the importance of the time period. A similar project could be accomplished during a discussion on Henry Clay—the great compromiser.

There doesn't need to be a formal school plan or center for independent studies. If necessary, independent studies can be conducted on a class level.

Teachers have been asking students to build their own project on a particular topic forever. Those second-grade projects on the fifty states are an independent study. Ever build an erupting volcano to represent Hawaii? Independent study.

On the high school level, students could build the volcano if they want as part of their presentation, but they can go further and examine the view the local Hawaiians have of the mainland Americans. Ever been referred to as a *haole* while vacationing in Hawaii? This would be a great study to enhance the chapter on U.S. imperialism.

CLOSING THOUGHT

A student who enjoys fashion could learn some business sense by linking with a local fashion entrepreneur. Not Social Studies, you say? It's total Social Studies. Students who thrive on their art courses need you. They need you to provide the skills to turn their love for art and fashion into a true business endeavor. You can be the bellows to their fire.

And finally, as stated by Randi Weingarten and Stanley Litow in their 2015 article in *U.S. News and World Report*, "Career and technical education, properly delivered, can provide a powerful link between school, college and career. It can motivate students through hands-on, project-based learning connected to interesting industries and careers."

Chapter Seven

Alternative Field Trips

Take a moment to envision two different courses.

The first course is a year-long class where you are responsible for teaching your students all about the U.S. government, from the Judiciary Act of 1789 to the battle of the Affordable Care Act of 2010. That's 221 years and thousands of events packed into one year. That's *Marbury v. Madison*, *Plessy v. Ferguson*, and *Roe v. Wade*. That's Washington, Jackson, Lincoln, Hayes, Roosevelt, Roosevelt, Kennedy, Reagan, and Obama. That's the Indian Removal Act, the Teapot Dome scandal, the Cuban Missile Crisis, Watergate, and Operation Iraqi Freedom.

The second course? Let's see, how about quarter-long course based on the 2016 presidential election. This alone would make for a great government course. Students would still have to learn some of the fundamentals of the U.S. government, but they'd see it in action. They'd see the actors. They'd feel the emotions and the divide in the country. They'd examine two very different candidates, both equally liked and disliked. This class is focused. This class is real. It has life.

Which sounds more interesting to you? Think of the students.

CHANGE FROM WITHIN

The current class system and schedule that most high schools use isn't going away anytime soon, but what other alternative courses can you construct outside the current class system? How about a week-long class over spring break? Or a week-long class over the summer? Perhaps you have an idea for a class that takes place a couple times a week during evening hours. Why not? Perhaps you can link up with local businesses, universities, or community centers to organize a course that focuses on depth.

Or maybe there's an overseas experience that you've been thinking about that'll just blow the students' minds.

Any school trip that goes abroad is going to be a memorable experience for a high school student. Just standing in the middle of Paris, staring down the Champs-Élysées at the Arc de Triomphe blows a kid's mind. But what if you add another layer for those students who are interested in international politics? And is there an alternative way for students who go on the trip to express what they learned, express who they talked with, what they saw and touched and smelled and felt?

How real of an experience can you build?

Let's say your topic is conflict or human rights. Where could your students actively engage with such topics?

There are few places on the planet that are fresh from conflict that are safe to travel to, but Kosovo is one of them. Not even two decades removed from a bloody war of Albanians killing Serbs and Serbs killing Albanians, Kosovo still simmers with tension, and though bad blood still exists, civility has replaced savagery. This country (or autonomous province, depending upon your position) still struggles in many ways, such as with its minority populations, economy, political control, education, and identity. So, why not take a trip with some students and provide a powerful case study in international affairs—a real-life study in how to establish democracy from the wounds of war.

How do you take an overseas trip and amp it up to something more than a passive experience?

LET THE THEME GUIDE YOUR IMAGINATION

When building an international trip experience for students, first select a theme. A trip to Kosovo could follow a theme *Growing Pains: War to Democracy.* Well in advance of the trip, begin making contacts with people and places in Kosovo who could make your students' adventure fulfilling and meaningful. It's best if you have a friend or colleague in a country who can help work some of the magic in the country, while you work it from abroad. Contact the U.S. embassy to get an outsider's view of things; the prime minister's office and local governments; the UN and their work to keep the peace; Mercy Corps and their work with the Roma populations; madrassas, so your students can experience a Muslim school; and local NGOs to learn their perspectives through their grassroots efforts.

At the home front, meet with students in pre-trip gatherings in order to lay the groundwork for what you expect from them on the trip.

How should you end an international experience? What should be the final product? What's the summative assessment?

Since students will be meeting with a variety of people face to face, stress to the students that it is their responsibility to become active, asking questions that pertain to the overall theme. Explain to students that they are taking on the role of photojournalists—documenting their interactions and observations through journal entries and photographs.

Following the trip, the students' photos and journals can be collected and put on display in a local gallery for the community to view.

As experts on the topic, students can speak to community groups, at schools, and at their own gallery opening. Students can talk about being invited into the house of the head of the local Roma community. Students could describe hearing about the collaboration between the Roma and Mercy Corps, as each works toward strengthening the village economics. Students could describe the colorful surroundings and the kids running around laughing. Students could comment on what they thought of the goals of the community.

This is education that will serve the students well down the road. This is education that will serve future employers well.

THE STRENGTH OF EXPERIENTIAL LEARNING

Students need to be able to think independently. In order to do that, we must provide them with opportunities to examine a subject first hand, outside of their comfort zone, beyond anything that they have observed before.

And get this: students can't cheat in experiential settings, nor would they want to, really. This is all about students observing, documenting their observations, and developing conclusions based on those observations.

Let's look at another possibility for students to experience their education.

The duty of a Social Studies teacher is to lead students toward being civically minded, engaged citizens, hopefully with a dab of ethics.

It takes a while to locate the overall goal of a Social Studies teacher. But after some searching, the National Curriculum Standards for Social Studies quotes itself saying ". . . the integrated study of the social sciences and humanities to promote civic competence." There a bunch of stuff that follows, but that first line captures the gist: bottom line, social studies teachers are supposed to guide students to take an active role in their community.

Consider the NCSS theme, culture. Within its description, it states, "Through experience, observation, and reflection, students will identify elements of culture as well as similarities and differences among cultural groups across time and place."

Hot dog! How perfect for what follows!

Again, let's work outside the classroom to accomplish our goal. What ready population exists that students could engage with and reflect upon while fulfilling a community need? How about "those in need"

SERVICE EXPERIENCES AND CIVIC DUTY

Every town, city, and village has a population in need. People across the United States are homeless, either chronically or situationally. Usually, they're ignored or just plain invisible to the rest of Americans who busily rush through their lives, but by working with people who are homeless, social studies teachers accomplish two goals:

1. They reach out and give a face to people who are often dismissed.
2. They provide their students with the opportunity to realize another world while engaging and helping.

How does it work? Well, it can work in many fashions, but what follows in one way to implement an experiential learning opportunity for your students. We'll use Archbishop Hoban's Project HOPE as our case study.

Each Wednesday after school, students, led by two teachers, gather in the school kitchen. Following all health code necessities (had to mention that), the team prepares food, usually simple sandwiches, chips, and cookies, or whatever the team feels like preparing or has on hand.

Once the group has organized the food and perhaps gloves and socks, they pile into the school van and head for downtown, where they'll stop along the railroad tracks, in the wooded areas, and alleyways.

A usual night goes like this:

The van stops at an intersection where a man is flying a sign that states his unfortunate circumstances. A few students exit the van with a bag of food and walk up to the man. The students begin a conversation. They know, from experience, that their goal is to engage. The food is secondary.

The experience is all about humanity. The students look their new friend in the eye, treating him as they should anyone, with respect. The students learn his name—in this case, Monty. The students learn about his situation and his past. They learn that Monty's situation and how he got to this point is different than the story they'll hear from Dave and Jess.

The students will hear many stories over the course of their time out on Project HOPE. They will discover that there is not a one-size-fits-all answer to homelessness. They'll learn that there is diversity out there, that each person has a different outlook and different goals. They'll learn that some people lost jobs, spouses, and houses. They'll learn that some people cope with alcohol and some don't. They'll hear perspectives on the city's answer to homelessness. They'll develop views of their own, and they'll learn that homelessness is much more complicated than the concept "bums are lazy," which, in itself, is a lazy assumption.

During Project HOPE, students develop communication skills and an appreciation for social capital. They gain insight into another's world—one they hopefully never have to experience, but one that will help provide them with a more well-rounded view of how the world works (or doesn't work).

Lights, camera, action. The students are on—it's time to perform. The teachers stand back, while the students take the lead.

There's no technology here. It's not necessary. This is not a virtual simulation of experiencing another world, another culture. Rather, the students are in the middle of it, on the front lines.

After trudging through a wooded area blanketed with snow, the team walks upon a city of tents circling a fire pit. The students are welcomed in, and they crowd around the fire. The students hear stories of why their new friends don't shack up in the local shelter. Students will hear about the newest book that a man is reading. Students will hear about why a couple doesn't get along with their parents. Students will meet with kids their age and men well into their sixties. Students will talk to people under the influence and people who have never had a drop of alcohol.

At the end of the evening, students share stories, reflecting on their experience and who they met, referring to each new friend by name.

Ultimately, the students act as ambassadors for the people who are homeless and the project itself. Once the bug hits the students, it'll spread rapidly through the community: to parents, stakeholders, and prospective students.

Promote that sucker, and it will pretty much fund itself.

INTERCONNECTED SCHOOLS

What if you build a field trip with another school? Get kids linked together. We do this with pen pals, linking students with counterparts overseas, but why not do it locally?

Give the students a task, working together to develop a solution to a problem. Perhaps teachers from different schools could decide on a handful of historical events the students need to work together to solve (the same could be done with modern events).

Teachers would develop folders filled with information regarding topics, similar to a document-based question (DBQ). Inside the envelope would be stuffed evidence, written sources, as well as pictures.

First, choose a theme for the day. For our purposes here, let's choose the Berlin Conference, 1884—the Scramble for Africa. Before the conference,

students are assigned countries and people to represent. The students' goals
are as follows:

1. Learn and understand their country's wants
2. Communicate with other students to set their agenda
3. Work toward fulfilling that agenda through negotiations and back-
    room deals

Unlike mock trial or Model UN, students work with students from another school to accomplish their tasks.

A simple itinerary might look as follows:

1. Participating students and teachers meet at the host school.
2. The first hour is spent through ice-breakers and team-building exer-
    cises, giving the students time to get to know one another.
3. The rules of the game are set, and the students begin their initial work
    learning about and discussing their country's goals at the conference.
    In addition to students acting as European countries, other groups of
    students will represent populations across Africa, such as in the Kongo
    Basin, the Asante of West Africa, or the Mahdist State.
4. Lunch—which would be superbly enhanced if it included ethnic
    foods. Students could bring their own or it could be catered by a local
    Ethiopian restaurant.
5. Following a meal that might include some back-door deals, student
    groups then dispatch their ambassadors to voice the platform of the
    others, taking into consideration economic, military, and political
    characteristics, not to mention nationalistic fervor.
6. The simulation can culminate with a large map of Africa on a screen
    for all to see, as students articulate their cases for what they believe
    they deserve, and what they are willing to do without. Students repre-
    senting African populations will express their distaste for the Africa
    being on the chopping block and how the negotiated borders might
    lead to disasters in the future.
7. The collaboration doesn't have to end after that one day. Students
    could remain in contact with their new friends at the other schools,
    consulting them on later projects.
8. If time, include a modern-day topic: gerrymandering, perhaps, or eth-
    nic divisions in Kenya.

POWER OF REFLECTION AND PROCESS

Any opportunity a student has to engage in an educational experience outside of the school building is beneficial. Traditional field trips fit this bill. But is there a way to take a field trip to the next level, so that it becomes a long-lasting, life-changing experience? How can teachers be sure that their students are taking something away from a field trip? That the students will act on what they learned from the field trip? That they will become more empathetic of others because they traveled to Kosovo? That they have a greater understanding of the complicated reality of homelessness?

Students benefit from reflecting on their experiences. Like someone working the clay before firing it up into a ceramic wonder, reflections give students the time to manipulate the experiences and concepts in their brains so that they truly understand.

In the book *Learning and Leading with Habits of Mind*, the authors explain how teachers are "facilitators of meaning making," and through the opportunity for reflection, teachers give their students the time to make meaning from their experience. Reflection puts the student in the position of becoming a producer as they synthesize the material in their head and produce something from understanding, rather than memorization. Thinking about thinking is a powerful tool.

Time is necessary when it comes to making meaning from a travel experience. Too often, time is dictated by the sequence of a textbook and some aged curriculum that speeds from unit to unit, blowing through the ages of history. Time needs to be wrestled back, trained or domesticated, if you will. Currently, time controls us, but we must wrangle it back so that we can take advantage of time. Too often, teachers cry, "There's not enough time"— students say the same. Give students time to reflect.

Guidance is also important. You're setting yourself up for disappointment if you ask your students, "Take out a piece of paper and reflect." Some guiding questions or structure is the key.

When it comes to field trips, try the Vowels of Travel: Start with "Why" and then elaborate with *I, O, E, U, A (Immerse, Observe, Engage, Understand, and Action)*. The Vowels take school trips to the next level, placing students at the forefront of the experience.

The order is critical.

Why. Why is this trip happening? As the teacher, why did you organize this experience? There has to be a clearly articulated purpose that can guide the students. And the biggest key: the teacher must be passionate about the experience. Create a *Why* that you believe in and that can positively impact the students for the long haul. Again, sightseeing experiences are awesome, but there is another level that a thoughtful *Why* can obtain and strengthen students' thinking skills.

Immerse. Again, a student in the action will get much more out of the experience than a student who is outside the action. A trip overseas that jumps from touristy spot to touristy spot is no doubt amazing but it misses the long-lasting and deep impact. Organize field trips where students get to go behind the scenes, where students can talk with the locals. Give students time to hear the perspectives of the locals.

Observe. Ask students to be present. There are plenty of distractions, especially if you are going to ask the students to journal or photograph their surroundings—these can pull the students from the experience. Guiding questions given to students prior to the experience can lead them into enhancing their awareness. What do the surroundings look like and why? How do the people interact with each other? What pictures or books are around? What are the people wearing? What are the perspectives of the locals?

Engage. It's easy for students to participate passively, viewing the experience, like they're watching a television program. Of course, there's a discomfort with engaging. Even in a room of teachers during a presentation, it's difficult to get participation—there's usually not an overwhelming number of raised hands and shouts of "Oh! Oh!" in an effort to be recognized. But there is a power in requiring students to step out of their comfort zone and engage. Students who engage will begin to feel the humanity in the experience, rather than just acting as a spectator who can remain distant from the subject.

Understand. In order for students to truly understand an experience, they'll have to take part—they'll have to engage. Students will have to discuss the subject and exchange ideas. They'll have to hear other perspectives. They'll have to journal about what they saw and felt. It's difficult to understand a scenario as an inactive participant. Students will have to have the time to manipulate the ideas and events in their head.

Action. Require your students to utilize what they have experienced and take action on it. This could be in the form of a project, a presentation, art, community work, whatever, so long as the students take action. By this point, they should be the experts on whatever it was that they experienced, and they should feel comfortable building something from it.

PLAYING THE REPORTER

Let's amp this up a bit. You and your students can record a podcast to post on iTunes or gather audio to be used for a local radio station.

Schedule podcasts with groups you meet with. Prior to the trip, ask the groups you have contacted if they would be willing to have your group record the conversation. The podcast can have the effect of organizing the conversation, preparing thoughts ahead of time, and ensuring that the students have an understanding about who they are meeting with.

Podcasts could be done on any level, local or abroad.

First ask students to practice by interviewing a family member, perhaps a grandparent about life during their childhood. For guidance, check out the StoryCorps website for questions to ask (https://storycorps.org/great-questions/).

Upon completion, students play their recorded interviews to the class. The interviews are kept short, maximum five minutes. With a simple goal of keeping the class's attention and being informative, the presentations are critiqued, which also provides students the opportunity to practice constructive feedback. All in all, students gain practice learning communication skills and open-ended questions. Students also learn to allow the conversation to flow. All too often, students use the questions they have written ahead of time to dictate the conversation flow, which potentially renders the student blind to possible interesting tangents.

CLOSING THOUGHT

It all comes down to real-life experiences. These can be done inexpensively, like with Project HOPE or interviewing grandparents. Real-life experiences can also be very expensive, such as international travel. Either price works. If you do decide to go the expensive route, then it's a good idea to research about fundraising options.

There are dozens of ways to raise money. A quick Google search will prove this. Choose the idea that works best for you and your students. Some ideas are better than others. I once thought I'd record an album with a fellow teacher, sell it on iTunes, and use the massive funds for an overseas trip. We basically made back the cost of recording the album.

Fundraisers work best when the students who the funds are benefiting are involved. Encourage the students to design a movie night or concert night, where food and drinks are available for purchase, where t-shirts are designed and sold, and where the students work the event. Such a fundraiser also gives students experience in event planning.

Chapter Eight

The Magic of Electives

It might be the elective that inspires a student. Perhaps it's the archaeology course, or the sociology one, or the summer course on sports teams. The more specific a course is, the more students can dive into it and make it real, becoming a part of the story. Moreover, the more specific a course is, the more a teacher can bring the content to life.

Traditional history courses span many years and many topics. Just as the students get the urge to step through the door to learn more, the door slams shut and you're on to the next subject.

Perhaps this unfortunate reality came to fruition when courses began following expensive textbooks, but now teachers can easily select from on-line sources whatever reading materials they want to complement a course.

Also, traditional Social Studies methodology follows a tenet that students have to learn the same history, and as a result, Social Studies teachers are asked to teach survey courses and are told, "We need to ensure a similar learning experience for every student." So, we've convinced ourselves to pump out the same thing every year, like Charlie Chaplin in *Modern Times*, robotically repeating the same movements at the conveyor belt.

We teach the same thing teachers taught ten years ago, and ten years before that, and even ten years before that—basically, since forever. Every student who has walked through the school doors over the past half-century has learned the same history, and year after year, teachers teach the same content, and we expect everyone to be excited about this. Social Studies needs enrichment!

Placing content as the top priority, rather than critical-thinking skills, is a blood-sucking fiend, draining the life from a history course.

But let's not get ahead of ourselves. The core courses won't change anytime soon, so let's play with what we've got and sprinkle some creative

and engaging electives into the curriculum, kind of like nutritionally fortify-
ing sugary cereal with vitamins that actually aide good health (of course, we
could just feed the kids whole foods, but we insist on this processed stuff,
like courses that cover all of world history).

SPORTS IN THE CLASSROOM?

You might be thinking, "A course on sports teams? Really?" Heck yes!
Think of the epic fun you could have with this class, while at the same time
challenging students to engage their historic thinking skills.

Let's say there was a class called Sports and Nicknames. Students choose
to look at the meaning behind team's names and logos. Take the Green Bay
Packers, for instance. A student who took on that case study would discover
the meat-packing industry, *The Jungle*, Theodore Roosevelt, and reforms in
big business. The student would also examine Green Bay itself and the public
ownership of the team.

On the other hand, a student who researches about the other football bay,
the Tampa Bay Buccaneers, would discover some very different, yet interesting, history. Here, a student would open the pages to the story of French
piracy against Spanish possessions in the Caribbean during the 1500s. Stories
of the Columbian Exchange and the conquistadors and the fate of the Arawak
people would emerge. A much different story than that of Green Bay, but an
equally interesting study that would use the same critical-thinking skills.

Or, travel across the country to the San Francisco Bay. Forty-Niners?
Well, that's an easy one. But what about the Giants? Why call a San Francisco team the Giants? Students who took on this challenge would find the New
York origins and also unravel evidence regarding the growing sports leagues
as they moved westward to follow growing markets and the growing airline
industry.

Why call a team in Salt Lake City the Jazz? Probably because they didn't
start in Utah. Are there any Cardinals in Phoenix? Not sure, but it is the state
bird of Illinois, which is where the football team originated. Is there music in
Nashville? Heck yeah! So name the triple-A team the Sounds and build a
scoreboard in the shape of a guitar with the innings running up the neck.

There are some team nicknames that make no sense. This could be an
opportunity for a student to modernize the name by arguing for one that has
some regional importance. The Cleveland Cavaliers come to mind, as do the
Toronto Raptors (but at least the Raptors can claim influence from pop
culture).

There's also the controversy that surrounds a number of team nicknames:
the Braves, Indians, and Redskins to name a few. This could make for a great
deliberation in class.

Courses that are focused not only help students organize their thoughts but also allow for deeper inquiry. They create real-life situations where students have to construct well-developed, reasoned decisions. Plus, they introduce an element of creativity.

As much as a school with all electives would address this reality, it doesn't exist (yet), and instead, a competition exists between elective courses and mandated core courses. There just isn't the time or teachers or money to do it all. But don't give up. There are alternatives a school and teachers can play around with.

Time on Our Side

As we know, schools need to meet the required number of instructional hours or days to fulfill state law. This number varies from state to state. How many instructional hours does it take to reach maximum student achievement? Who knows, and who cares really, because it's more about the quality of those hours than the number.

The instructional time has to pack a punch or it's not worth it.

Worldwide, countries also differ on the number of instructional hours, and there's no correlation between what we might consider the strongest education systems and hours. So, rather than increase the hours, burning out our teachers, why not focus on the strength of fewer hours.

Think of the workplace. More than ever, employees are working from home. Employers are finding that their employees can be just as productive, if not more so, by embracing a more flexible work environment. There's very little an office employee does at her place at work that she couldn't do on her own computer and phone at home or a cafe.

Why demand employees stay at the office when they have essentially completed what they need to do at the office?

Let's free up the time and become more creative with the instruction.

In Nathaniel Koloc's article, "Let Employees Choose When, Where, and How to Work," he talks about how freedom equals productivity. Both the employee and employer benefit from freedom. Koloc refers to his own company, ReWork, where his staff has time to work remotely, and some have done so from overseas.

It works for adults. Does freedom work for students? Can students handle a lack of structure that doesn't hold them in check, five days of the week for eight hours a day in order to finish their work? Kids in Finland do.

Freedom can be a powerful thing (as many Americans know). Students today don't need a classroom to accomplish their work necessarily, unless that work is an active, engaging, experiential one. Anya Kamenetz writes in her article, "High School 'Work From Home Day' Gives Students Taste of

Independence" that students are free to learn in the environment of their choosing during a stay-at-home day. If the kid wants to listen to music to do her work, fine. If the student wants to do his work while sitting at a local cafe, fine. The stay-at-home style doesn't work for some students, but it might just be exactly what others need.

Is the setting we stuff kids in out of date? Might there be more motivating atmospheres for the future generations? There isn't a one-size-fits-all answer, and that's part of the issue. We're moving into a reality where the concept of an office or workspace is becoming more malleable.

Rethink the Use of Hours

Does your school necessarily have to go far beyond the required instructional hours mandated by the state? Consider scaling back on going well over the number of hours your school is in session for the traditional schedule. Again, it's how that time is used, not the number of hours.

Let's use those *extra hours* for something engaging and motivating.

In any case, some schools meet well beyond the minimum number of instructional time—enough that a school could get creative with those *extra hours* if it wanted.

Do something with your extra time. Take a week and create a non-traditional experience for students. Do all students need to participate? That's a question your school can answer itself. Remember, you could build a course specifically on the 2016 presidential race. Maybe it's just an intensive week-long course.

Some schools offer a senior experience, and that's fantastic, but why not offer something for *all* students? Plus, there are a handful of sophomores who could outperform a handful of seniors. Give those sixteen-year-olds a chance to gain a college-like experience or college credit.

You want to build a specialty course to fill some of your *extra time*? Some specialty courses take some outside help, some community involvement. There's an entire resource out there for schools: experts in the community. A successful course and a successful school district is going to be one that collaborates with the community—a sort of synergetic education. The future needs to be one where the entire community takes part in the education of its youth. And why not? An educated population is a population that can give back to the community.

Let's build a quick curriculum with the community. Consider a summer course. Some students won't be interested in a week or two-week summer course, but if it's specific enough, and exciting enough, and engaging enough, then you might just get enough students to join the ride.

Again, the goal for the Social Studies is to challenge students with problems to solve and real-life experiences. Very few of our students who are interested in history will enter the profession of history teacher or museum curator. Many will use their well-rounded thinking skills to enter business or law or advertising or event coordinating or, or, or. . . .

There are plenty of people in your community, including parents of students, who are involved in business. As a result, you could develop a summer week-long course or "Quick Course" on business, inviting volunteers from the business community to share their expertise with the students. There are hundreds of businesses, so diversify the course with a mix of different industries.

How about this schedule:

- Monday: *Introduction and finding a niche.* Students are tasked with the challenge of finding a niche and selling an idea in a sort of business challenge. What the students will learn this week will provide them with tools to build a viable plan. A guest speaker today could be someone associated with a local foundation that provides grants for innovative business ideas. Students will talk with a different entrepreneur each day. Throughout the week, students will be given time to consult other students and hear feedback.
- Tuesday: *Marketing, online sales, social media.* Walk away with a website, social media campaign, and insight on how to brand themselves and their ideas.
- Wednesday: *International.* Today's guest could speak on the importance to think global or perhaps speak to the students about alternative ideas overseas that could be used as inspiration locally—think bike lanes in Copenhagen. Students could also learn about types of personalities and the skills needed in building relationships. Are they a lion or a peacock?
- Thursday: *The Arts: performing and visual.* Today's visitor explains the power of place and what businesses are looking for in a location. Safety and cost of living top that list, but cultural strength is huge too. The added benefit of the arts, no matter if it's outdoor art or the symphony, strengthens neighborhoods and a city as a whole. Students will learn about grassroots efforts to establish pop-up shops, as well as encouraging outreach events at the local museum. How strong cultural basis and arts attract businesses. Small business leaders and organizations that help promote small businesses. Pop-ups. Invigorating a community's economy using different strategies.
- Friday: *Presenting the business plan.* Students have time to fine-tune their business plan by discussing their ideas with the other students and finalizing their presentation. Invite local experts to sit on a panel to listen and provide feedback.

LEARNING FROM EXPERTS

It's not a business course based in terminology, balance sheets, or the stock market. So you ask, "Where's all the rigor?"

The rigor is in the real-life stories and experiences from experts, as they offer advice and fuel inspiration. The rigor is in the students working through building a business plan, building a website, building a marketing plan, building a sales page on the website, building an elevator speech, building a vision, and then selling their plan by the end of the course.

The course is about engaging with experts, practicing skills, implementing those skills, thinking creatively, working with experts to iron out kinks, and presenting their business to a panel of experts. These are college and career-readying skills.

The Innovation Incubator Department

So how does one coordinate all of this? It's difficult for a teacher or even a school's social studies department to coordinate all of the community outreach necessary to build a successful collection of non-traditional courses. No doubt, it can be done, but could you make it a school-wide effort so that more are on board?

To manage independent studies, alternative field trips, and the Quick Courses, a school could invest in an Innovation Incubator—a department that solely focuses on organizing the many real-life experiences the school offers the students.

This is done on an increasing basis at the college level, and many high schools have senior experiences. Schools have experiential learning programs, internship partnerships, on-site opportunities. Some schools even have a specific focus. For instance, Akron Public Schools is rolling out academies, where each of the high schools in the area focus on a particular curriculum. One school is centered on health care, which fits nicely with the strong health care providers in the area, making the content relevant.

Schools create real-life experiences for students because they simulate real-life environments that prepare students for creative and critical thinking skills that colleges and employers demand.

The director or directors of the Innovation Incubator (or call it whatever you like: The Simulator sounds pretty cool) act as liaisons between the wealth of expertise in the community and students' interests.

How can younger students take part in such an opportunity if they can't drive? Or where will students find the time? Or how can I let my kid venture off on his own into a foreign part of town for hours?

There's always ways around barrier questions like these.

It's fine to expect students to fulfill their Innovation work on their own time. It's fine to group students in teams, where the members can collaborate. This might make it easier to fulfill their community engagement or on-site research. Also, not every moment of the students' Innovation experience has to be on location—perhaps they are required five site visits a semester. Bottom line: if a school wants it to happen, they can make it happen.

Think of the Innovation Incubator as a sort of action academy. Its goal is to engage students, to make them participating members of society. In doing so, it's important that the Incubator builds relationships with experts in the community. The Director would become a face at local events, even organizing events at the school.

Not all Innovation experiences have to be off campus. The Innovation Incubator would invite local experts to speak at the school, a sort of Experts Experience. Students, as well as parents, would be invited for an evening presentation and discussion of ideas.

Invite experts from the community to teach an evening course at the school twice a week. There are so many great Social Studies subjects that could tap into the expertise of the local population. Combine a few themes together: economic stimulation + neighborhood revitalization + social media = awesome course.

The awesome course would be led by an expert (or several) in urban development—or team the person up with a business leader. The course could look at strategies used to help revitalize cities, researching success stories from around the country. First, students would propose solutions, and then they would invent a marketing campaign to educate the community. Bring in local leaders to judge the final results.

CLOSING THOUGHT

Electives are a bit more palatable for students—they're usually easily digestible topics, unlike the mishmash of unrelated topics in a World History course. It's difficult to comprehend, and therefore remember, the important details of the French Revolution one week and the details of the Imperialization of Africa the next, and then to have to memorize for the final. Well, that's all it is: memorization. Nicely organized, focused topics don't have to be memorized. There's no need to binge it the night before a test, because the story flows. It makes sense to the cognitive abilities of a high school student.

Chapter Nine

I Didn't Learn This in College, Either

RECEIVED E-MAIL #1

I just wanted to thank you for your recent article, "Why Do Students Hate History?" in EdWeek. *I'm currently student teaching in a Newark, NJ, high school and already I can pick up from my students that they find the content irrelevant.*

If you're not too busy, I'd like to know a little more about how you conduct your thinking skills lessons, so that I can better reflect on my practice as a social studies teacher.

Thanks in advance for your response, and I look forward to hearing back from you.

RECEIVED E-MAIL #2

I just read your article in Education Week, *all I can say is AMAZING!*

I am a non-traditional teacher, meaning I went to college in my thirties after ten years in the US Army, I went through the Ohio Troops to Teachers program, and I now teach at Metro Early College Middle School.

I just had a discussion with my principal and fellow SS teachers about how to squeeze 750 BC–1600 AD into a school year, and by the way I only have them M-W-F for social studies.

I love your concept and I too hated hearing in college "You are a History major, I hated history!"

So far my kids tell me they love social studies and the way I tell it as a story and all the side information I give them that is not in textbooks (I must being doing something right). After reading your article I feel better about how I am instructing my kids. Thank you again for writing it!

History Rocks!

Turning an Appliance Manual into an Epic Novel

The teachers above have heart and drive, and they want to turn their students' experience into something relevant and special. It sounds like they have a good read on their students, and their students find the textbook history a little drab. It also sounds like these teachers have a true desire to spice things up, and they realize it's going to involve moving beyond the status quo.

We need to reach out to young or new teachers and hear them out. They have questions and ideas. They're not dim. They know things could be different. Why not let new teacher enthusiasm shine? We shouldn't stifle it.

It's not easy to develop new ideas and approaches to education while on the job. As a teacher, a grunt on the front lines, there isn't a great deal of time to innovate, collaborate, and challenge the status quo—that's usually set aside for people who aren't teaching.

Young teachers have the greatest opportunity to innovate. They have the energy and they haven't usually taken on a great number of added responsibilities. However, young teachers are busy trying to figure out what the heck they're supposed to be doing. They're fine-tuning the basics, juggling classroom management, content, differentiated instruction, school policies, as well as just how to strategize restroom breaks.

Just as a teacher begins to become comfortable with the job, let's say three years in, the school will turn to that teacher to carry a heavier load of courses and responsibilities.

Teachers are tapped to advise student council or coach a sport or monitor a club or take part in a committee or play department chair, or something.

Just as teachers are ready to start innovating their courses into something engaging that motivates students, they are pulled in another direction.

Saying *yes* is a positive thing; however, overusing yes can get a teacher into trouble, even douse the flame of education.

DATA DATA DATA

Data is a very powerful tool, and it provides a lot of answers, but humans are unpredictable creatures that need individual attention, and we can't forget that.

The majority of students got a question wrong on a test? That's a red flag to do a little research on that question or content, and that's a form of data that's helpful. Your tenth graders as a whole scored low on the reading part of the ACT? Well, that's a sign that you might want to focus on some literacy strategies for the school.

Data's great. Football fans use it for their fantasy teams. The military uses it to determine the success of a mission. The local cafe uses it to determine whether or not to stay open on Saturday afternoons. Wall Street uses it to play with money. And teachers use it to ensure that students understand what it is they're supposed to be understanding.

As great as data is, it's not all-powerful.

In the 2011 article, "Why Are Finland's Schools Successful," author Lynnell Hancock quoted a principal in Finland who said, "If you only measure the statistics, you miss the human aspect." Bingo! This is pure music to educators' ears.

We need to keep in mind that data only tells so much, especially about people, because people are inconsistent.

The Big Why

For the purpose of this book, the author sent out a survey to students at the University of Akron who were studying to become Social Studies teachers. What follows are two very different responses from young, aspiring teachers to a variety of questions.

Response #1

1. **Why do you want to be a Social Studies teacher?**
   I have always had an interest in history and the government so I thought what better way would I talk about all this than to teach a younger generation!
2. **What would the greatest class lesson look like to you?**
   The greatest class lesson would start out with notes on a subject, then doing some sort of handout over the content to lock in the knowledge.
3. **What's your vision of an ideal school that would stimulate student understanding?**
   N/A
4. **Concerns you might have about inspiring students to "buy-in" to a particular unit of study.**
   There are many students who do not care about learning in general—what is your way of making the kids want to learn? Or how do make them question and learn the content the best?
5. **Any questions about the reality of teaching high school?**

If you had the opportunity to start college over, would you still become a social studies teacher?

Response #2

1. **Why do you want to be a Social Studies teacher?**

   Ever since my high school experiences, especially that in AP U.S. history, and further in college, I have wanted to bring my love for social studies to as many people as I can and do so in a fun, engaging way as I had experienced. All too often I hear about and see students' dislike of the social studies, and I want to change that stigma.

2. **What would the greatest class lesson look like to you?**

   The greatest class lesson to me would be one where students are leading their own learning and the desire to learn more about the topic is sparked by their inquiry while I or the educator takes the role of guide on their learning adventure.

3. **What's your vision of an ideal school that would stimulate student understanding?**

   An ideal school for me would be one where students are encouraged to make mistakes, take risks, and experience failures in an environment where they can do so without fear of negative repercussions and have a multitude of opportunities to learn from their experiences.

4. **Concerns you might have about inspiring students to "buy-in" to a particular unit of study.**

   My biggest concern and challenge is/has been to relate topics of study to every student and make it relevant to their lives today. This is a big push in social studies and is one of the most challenging aspects of teaching for any content area.

5. **Any questions about the reality of teaching high school?**

   Being a high school teacher, is it more important to teach the content or prepare students with skills they will use the rest of their lives?

Let those different responses simmer internally for a moment.

LEARN FROM A TEACHING VETERAN

Now, let's contrast those e-mails from young educators that opened this chapter with a section that tells the story of a veteran educator.

Rob Yanko has taught Social Studies for forty-four years. Forty-four freaking years!

And somehow he's kept his classes fresh and real.

When the seniors write their memories in the school paper, Mr. Yanko appears frequently. The kids love his classes. And they're AP classes!

How can this be? What's Rob's secret?

First, let's try to encapsulate Rob's personality. Before becoming a teacher, Rob played in a band in clubs around Kent State University. In fact, he was playing a show when the ROTC building was burned by protesting students in 1970. He hasn't set the guitar down.

Rob uses his musical talents to bring history to life. He'll play "The Battle of New Orleans" or Woody Guthrie's "This Land Is Your Land." He'll use the musical numbers to get students thinking about characters in the song or events surrounding the song's subject. Take "New Orleans" for instance. The song's content nicely sets the stage for the battle itself, but you can ask the students to take a step back and try to explain more.

What was the War of 1812 about? Why did the War Hawks push for it? How did it impact General Jackson's career? Why did the Americans defeat the British in New Orleans? Cotton makes an appearance in the song. Does it play a role in the war? And why the heck is there an alligator in the lyrics? Through whose perspective is the song written? And why, in the name of all that is rock 'n' roll, did Johnny Horton's version of the song rise to number one on the charts in 1959? What was going on then?

So many questions can be asked and answered through songs.

Rob also takes his talents outside of the classroom. Each year he writes new lyrics to a humorous song and plays it at a school-wide assembly. The goal of the song is to make the students laugh and sing along, as his stinging lyrics take jabs at teachers and the administration. [1]

Rob is young at heart. That's his personality, so that's how he approaches teaching.

"You have to be true to yourself," he says during a chat over a couple beers, and he goes on to explain that his approach to teaching might not be the same way another successful teacher approaches it.

"I see teaching as almost improvisational theater," Rob explains.

It must work for him. His longevity, positive outlook, and connection with the students are proof that it works.

He admits he's not a curriculum person. His cup of tea (or beer) isn't building creative semester-long projects. He's much more comfortable as a sort of conductor, a musical conductor.

Rob is a storyteller, and he stresses the importance of presenting history to students in the form of a story.

He remembers his high school years, when history was often presented as names and dates, making it difficult for him to find meaning or get excited about the class. From that experience, he came to the conclusion that there must be another way to teach history.

In his approach, Rob includes the students in his story telling. He doesn't place the students in the story, but he requires their participation in telling the story, in giving it depth.

Rob teaches AP European History. One of the topics he covers with the students is the Protestant Reformation. He'll tell the story of Henry VIII and his battle with Pope Clement VII in pieces. He'll start the story by giving very little of the story, asking students whether or not the pope should grant the annulment. The students undoubtedly say that Henry should be granted his request. As Rob gives a little more of the story, the students begin to rethink their certainty. The more information Rob provides, the more complex the story becomes. With every page of the story, Rob goes around the room, asking for advice from the students—nothing too complicated, just something quick that keeps them engaged and alert. By the end, the room has been turned into an orchestra of sorts, each student playing their role to make the story come to life.

Rob also enjoys using his body as a human map. He'll describe his torso as the United States, being sure to point out Ohio as his left nipple. Florida is his left thigh, and I won't explain where Texas is. The point is, despite its ridiculousness, the students don't forget the story of the map.

Sure, Rob throws document-based questions after document-based questions at his AP students, but even then, there's a story to be built—that's what a DBQ is building, a story.

Rob's students score well on the AP exams. His style works . . . for him.

"You have to be true to yourself," Rob warns.

Don't deny yourself your own skills. Those are the ones that will come out naturally in a classroom. The students can tell when you're trying to be something else.

To be fair, it's not easy to be yourself as a first-, second-, or third-year teacher (or even beyond). You're still trying to figure out the monster—that elusive monster—but some of the times, the monster is you.

"There's only so much you can do content-wise in a day." Another line from Rob's mantra.

Is teaching all about personality?

Rob talks about the importance of learning the personality of the students. Each class has its own personality, its own chemistry. There's a human component to teacher that Rob subscribes to. It's important for students to score well on tests, but knowing what makes each student's brain and heart tick is equally paramount.

You could argue that Rob's style is very teacher-centered. Is that wrong? Given how much his students enjoy his classes and how well they do on their AP exams, it would be hard to argue that Rob's technique is wrong.

Rob is a facilitator, building the Social Studies story through the help of the students' excited participation, but his skills evolved over years of fine-tuning and adapting. He had to learn and struggle through a lot before he perfected his art.

And what if Rob had a chance to talk to his younger self?

> During my first year I always felt inadequate because it seemed I was barely hanging on and only staying one page—at times one paragraph—ahead of the students in their history books. I would advise myself to, as quickly as possible, get to the stage where you know what you want the students to understand at the end of the unit or semester or year. I guess it helps to know the end of the story before you start the story.

Rob's classes are also challenging classes. He expects a lot from his students, and teachers will see a great return when they make it clear to their students that they have confidence enough in their students to tackle demanding work.

Kids know what busy work is, and they'll treat it as such. But give them a high-stakes task, and they're liable to rise to the occasion, not sink to the level of busy work. In the article, "Raising Urban Students' Literacy Achievement by Engaging in Authentic, Challenging Work," authors Teale and Gambrell explain the benefits of, well, authentic and challenging work for students. Their paper, among many others, mentioned the role that professional learning communities (PLC) can have on building a coherent plan for addressing student needs and best practice.

Most often, these PLCs take place within the schools. But what about a PLC that consists of teachers from several schools?

Our schools can get pretty insular, where we learn from a small pocket of people, branching out only during conferences. Rather than thinking small, think big. Utilize the entire education community where you live. There are hundreds of great teachers where you live. Seek them out!

How about creating your own PLC? Get to know some social studies teachers from other schools. Build an enjoyable group of those whose ideas excite you and whose feedback fuels you.

CUSTOMIZING YOUR OWN PLC

Time is a scarce resource. It's difficult to make room in your busy schedule for work outside of work. We'd much rather distance ourselves from work while "not on duty." This is totally understandable. But what if the outside-of-work work was fun?

There's Avon, Mary Kay, Tastefully Simple, Trades of Hope, but why not a sort of MLM (mid-level marketing) for Social Studies teachers, where project ideas and success stories are shared? Organize a group of cool cats you want to hang out with and shoot the Social Studies on a Tuesday evening. Someone host, someone bring the food, someone bring the drinks, and someone bring more drinks because you know the one guy will forget.

Like a book club, come prepared to share new ideas or, if you have questions, bring those. Take selfies, laugh, get off topic, but use the carefree time to share.

In a way, it's the anti-PLC. There's no collection of data. There's no focus. There's no school building. And everyone wants to be there.

Make it enjoyable so it doesn't seem forced or a waste of time. Call it a Social Studies Swag or History Hang or Wine Not Work.

Here are a couple fun ideas from a recent Social Studies Swag outing:

• St. Vincent—St. Mary's High School in Akron, Ohio has its own victory garden. Yep. That's right. The school received a grant to fund the idea of building a garden in an empty lot. The idea was to create a livable classroom, where students would learn about plants and conservation and food and everything else you can do with a garden. Students led the way, assisted by staff and others, bringing the school together in a worthwhile and forward-thinking project.

The plot sits enclosed, so it's functional during the long Akron winters, and it makes for a good reminder of great education as one drives by it on West Market Street.

The school has tried to intertwine all of the curriculums into the garden, and what better way for the Social Studies department to make it work than to use it as a teaching tool when discussing World War II.

Yeah, yeah, World War II was about war, and the United States ended up victorious overseas, but sometimes we forget to spend time on the homefront—the ball bearings, the synthetic rubber from Akron, and the victory gardens.

If you think about it, there's quite a few ways to link the garden into a history class. There was Jefferson's agrarian democracy. There's the feudal domains of the European Middle Ages. There's the whole Thanksgiving story—whatever that was.

The garden, whether the focus is science or history, is an interactive tool, a hands-on learning experience.

CLOSING THOUGHT

A fellow teacher and I decided to start a podcast, Recess, with the goal of talking with other teachers, administrators, and community educators. We wanted to learn more. What do others do? We talked with superintendents, museum educators, math teachers, art teachers, Social Studies teachers, and whomever was willing to talk with us. All of the conversations were inspirational and humbling, really. We talked with the mayor of our town to learn his thoughts, and we learned from a local barista. We can learn from everybody. There are ideas out there. Don't limit yourself.

NOTES

1. There have been a couple times where Rob has been chastised for his words at assemblies. He brushes it off, all in good fun.

Chapter Ten

Embrace the Struggle

Nelson Mandela said, "I never lose. I either win or learn." That is the mindset shift students need.

Picture this: You're in the middle of a great class discussion. Students are asking genuinely curious questions. Other students are offering suggestions to their classmates. The class is moving swiftly. Things are popping. Then Micah raises his hand.

"Will this be on the test?"

Everyone pauses as they wait for your response.

Micah poses an aggravating but legitimate (and yet perceptive) question. The test is how students are judged, so why wouldn't that be their primary concern?

Students have plenty of tests, all of which are key to graduating to the next level. All of which are used to rate the students against other students. With tests carrying so much weight, why should students take interest in something that won't be on the tests? It just doesn't jibe with the system students are trudging through.

The shortest route between two points is a straight line. The students know that getting from point A to B is the goal. The test (point B) is the goal. Students wonder, *"What's the fastest route to the end?"* Elaborations or side conversations are not important.[1] They might think rest stops or side trips that *won't be on the test* will slow the class toward its ultimate goal—the test!

But side trips are where the adventures occur, uncovering the unknown, and learning occurs, too. Side trips aren't marked on the map with the ink that identifies the route from A to B, but there is so much to learn with a stop that's not part of the map—the curriculum map. In fact, there's even more to discover when you stray from the ink line than from staying on the ink line.

Step off the line!

Can you imagine going on a road trip without pulling into a rest stop? Even if you don't care to take in a breath of the world where you stopped the car, your bladder will be happy. It's kind of necessary. Of course, there are inventive and acrobatic ways around stopping.

What if Jason just found the Golden Fleece, and that's where the story ended? What if he and the Argonauts didn't endure fantastic adventures? Sure, lives would have been spared, but the story certainly wouldn't have lasted the ages. And yes, the whole point of the epic adventure was to reach the fleece—that's how they gauged their success—but the route, the blood, the sweat, the perseverance illustrated the importance of the fleece.

How do we encourage the students to embrace the path to the goal as much as the goal itself? How do you get beyond the *just get it over with* mentality?

STRAIGHT LINES AREN'T INTERESTING

Much of Social Studies is about the process, the skills developed during the quest for a solution. What if, for the sake of time, Sir Conan Doyle left out the part where Sherlock Holmes and Dr. Watson work through the clues and near-death experiences and just wrote the part where Holmes explains who committed the crime? Sure, it might be a quick read, but all the adventure and amazement would be missing. The stuff that keeps the readers coming back is the stuff in between the beginning and end—the path.

You need skills in venturing onto the path in the real world. Failing is part of the process—working through the trudge and seeing the complications.

And the Social Studies are perfect for the path. There's a lot of gray in the Social Studies.

The fact of the matter is that there really aren't straight lines to the answer. In real life, the path to the end is a squiggly one, running here to there, above and below, and even backward sometimes. There is no A to B, the end. *Forget about it!*

Social Studies are not clean, easy, or simple. The hope is that students see an event from a different perspective. The hope is that students understand how complicated a decision can be. The hope is that students understand how many pieces there are to the Social Studies puzzle.

The Social Studies teacher's goal is to help students move beyond "just blow 'em up" and "just split it up." Those are unreasonable, unsatisfactory, and unrealistic decisions.

EMBRACE THE PATH

Many of the answers our students seek in school can be found on their phone or online. Just ask your phone or computer, "What is the importance of Social Studies?" and it can give you an instant answer. *Ask.com* tells us "Social Studies is important because it teaches students fundamental concepts of culture, economics and politics skills to groom them into educated, productive citizens." Print that on a piece of paper and hand it in! A+!

It's the *skills* that are important, however. That's the foundation of the Social Studies, and the skills are gained on the path toward the goal.

It's no secret to you that Social Studies studies society. It's also no secret that society is unpredictable. It's also no secret that people are unpredictable because people are. People are just plain strange. People aren't constant. Their moods change from moment to moment. A person on Monday might make a different decision about something than they would on Friday, and in between is anyone's guess. (People are bad guessers about people too.)

Bottom line: the Social Studies examine a very gray subject. Ideologies might think in blacks or whites, but people don't act in blacks and whites.

And that's the key—the Social Studies help provide those real life-skills that are needed to endure the gray reality of the world. Social Studies teachers exist to help lay the foundation for making decisions, interacting with others, maintaining order, strengthening ethical behavior, contributing to society, running a business, breaking a code, defending against an enemy, and convincing an ally, and, well, every other social behavior.

So, reducing the Social Studies to an A to B mentality defeats the entire purpose of the discipline.

THE PROCESS

In Nathan Barber's 2014 article "Focus on the Process and Results Will Follow," he writes that a "focus on the process can yield several benefits for students, including fostering a growth mindset, creating a student-centered environment, and reducing stress for students."

He's right. The only problem is that students aren't familiar with such a system. Their motivator is the final grade.

"How many points is this?"

"When's the test?"

"How many pages should this be?"

This is what the system has conditioned students to ask.

But Social Studies teachers have the perfect tools to fix this. Our job is to strengthen the skills that are associated with the process. The biggest challenge now is to re-program the students, make them comfortable with placing the points second and the process first.

Say to the students, "Like a tortilla chip for guacamole, the content will act as a vehicle for the skills. Our focus is the skills, the process toward finding the answer."

For the students to buy into this process-over-points mentality, the teacher will have to buy in too. Social Studies teachers will have to allocate time for explaining that the process is prime. The students need to trust the teacher, so the shift toward the process over the points can't be half-ass.

For the teacher to make the switch from points to process, there's a few lesson priorities that will have to be built into the curriculum of a Social Studies course.

1. *Beginning-of-the-year explanation.* And you're going to have to sell this. Put on your best cult of personality charismatic hat, and convince those kids.

2. *Practice the process.* Start with a current event, something most students will be familiar with. The content for an initial practice doesn't matter. Think of the introductory assignment as training camp, not a regular season assessment.

3. *Consistency.* There has to be opportunities for the students to build their process skills throughout the year or semester. Just as important, the teacher has to provide valuable feedback to the students. Are they on the right track?

4. *Grade progress.* The students are still grade-hungry, so place a greater emphasis on progress than on homework or quizzes. How do you grade progress, you ask? Well first, we have to answer the question *What skills should the students master?* Are you more interested in inquiry skills or presentation skills or collaborative skills?

   Maybe you just want to focus on one skill a quarter. Maybe you want to leave it up to the students to decide what skill they want to build. Make it work for you and your students. Perhaps you'll find that the skill you feel your students need to work on is not the same skill for students in another district, or another class.

5. *Grading progress?* Provide opportunities for the students to reflect on the learning process. Let them explain their process to you and each other. Grade student reflections. Ask them to write down or vocalize questions about the process. Give students a question and the answer and ask them to explain how they fit. Give the students a multiple choice question and the answer, and ask them to explain why it's the answer. Ask students to explain how they went about finding the answer. What did they think? Where did they look?

WHAT SKILLS?

We should probably take a moment to define some skills that students in a Social Studies course should master. Maybe the students will master them all during the course of the year, or maybe you select a couple, or maybe there's a skill you feel the students at your skill need to work on, given a standardized test or given your own observation. To get you started, here's a short list of skills:

1. *Historical context.* Provide the students with a primary resource to read. Ask them to focus solely on the context of the event described in the resource. What else is occurring at the time? What occurred prior to this event? This helps stretch the students' brains beyond the immediate. If the students read about the Korean uprising of 1919, you could ask them to put the event in context with the Treaty of Versailles, or you could require them to compare the uprising to other protests of 1919, such as the Amritsar Massacre.

2. *Point of view and biases.* Ask the students to focus on the author of an article. Ask the students to try to read into the perspective of the author. Who is the author associated with? What ideology does the author subscribe to? If the students are reading the *Federalist Papers*, you can ask the students to see if they can figure out what bias the author has regarding the role of government.

3. *Make connections.* Ask students to pair up and give each a different article to read or video to watch. When they are finished with their respective work, the students share what their reading or video was about, and then they have to figure out how the two relate to the unit at hand, or how the two fit with each other. Perhaps one student reads about the September 11, 1973, overthrow of Allende in Chile, while the partner reads about Nicaragua and the battle between the Sandinistas and Contras. The unit, of course, is the Cold War.

4. *Purpose of the author.* Keep an eye out for when the *New York Times* op-eds stories. These are just fantastic, and sometimes they're even written by a country's leader. U2's lead singer Bono wrote one that was printed April 12, 2016. In it, Bono writes about the need to embrace the people fleeing the violence in Syria. He challenges Europe to see the refugees as assets, instead of burdens. He calls on the Western world to act. From the article, students can learn something about the refugee crisis and the refugee camps. Perhaps students can go further and examine Bono's excursion into various refugee camps. Students can then dig into Bono's past to see who he is and other causes he has supported. Students would find his ONE campaign and his push for

debt forgiveness of African countries, and students would find that the superstar, no doubt, has a purpose.

5. *Intended audience.* There's something about those public service announcements from the 1950s that just call out, "Please use me in a Social Studies course!" Ask your students to watch a few and determine who they are for. Is the video about leading your livestock to your barn during a nuclear strike intended for the same audience as the video that calls on kid to duck and cover? Another great way to exercise this is to ask students to watch campaign speeches of a single candidate. Does the candidate say the same thing in West Virginia as he does in Florida?

6. *Irony and satire.* This is a little harder, but can students pick up on humor or irony? In Jonathan Swift's *A Modest Proposal*, he mocks the greed and abundance of the wealthy by suggesting that the poor sell their babies as food for the rich. Reading this at face value is a nonsensical absurdity. Can students discover what motivates Swift to write such a disgusting proposal?

7. *Share.* This is one of the hardest parts. Can students take those swirling ideas in their head and release them from their mouth in a coherent and concise and convincing way? Start small on this one. Can students build an elevator speech about a protest for rights in Russia in 1905? Can students tweet 140 characters that express the thesis of whatever they just read? Can students focus on the point of their talk without being distracted with useless information? Hold up a card that reads *Causes of the Renaissance*, and everything a student says must address that one point. Then, as the next student stands to present, hold up a new card that reads another point. The student has to stay on point. If she starts telling you the year Martin Luther was born then redirect her.

Once the students master these skills through passive means, such as reading and watching videos, the students can take it on the road. Ask the students to conduct an interview of their choosing. Once the interview is completed, ask the students to address the interview using their newly mastered Social Studies skills. Beware, however. The students just might start analyzing you!

CLOSING THOUGHT

A shift from points to process takes time. It's quite time consuming to help all twenty-five or thirty students in a class build their skills. It's much easier to grade multiple-choice questions that assess content memorized. So, once again time becomes an issue.

Since time is an issue, perhaps you can include two or three times in a semester where you explain to students that the focus is on the process.

Another idea is to use groups. When students work in groups, stress that their skills will be assessed. That way you can have consultations with seven or eight groups, rather than thirty students.

When focusing on the process, you will have to start with some baseline data. Where is each student at regarding skills? Do you match struggling students with students who are well beyond their years? Do you match students of similar skills in groups? These questions are for you to decide. What's your preference and philosophy?

NOTE

1. Of course, getting a teacher off topic is one of the goals of a class—a joyous event, even. But distracting a teacher and a class discussion that elaborates on a topic are rather different. But if you can make a class discussion seem like the kids got you off topic, you're good.

Chapter Eleven

Build a Book

Texts are everywhere. There's the traditional hardback text in the classroom. There's the e-text on students' mobile devices. There's the text your student just sent his buddy during class. And there's the hundreds of supplementary materials students and teachers can find online.

Social Studies textbooks make for good organizational tools. They walk students from unit to unit, bolded headings, stressing important terms, giving heads up of what's to come, and using the same stock photos used in the previous two editions. [1]

Texts act as a reference to students. No doubt. But do they have to be so cumbersome in length and lifeless in character?

A Social Studies text cannot be all-inclusive. There is just too much to write about. Of course, there can't be a million-page book. Think of the assigned readings, not to mention the clogged hallways with students dragging their hundred-pound books from class to class.

Enter, the conundrum: What is the correct balance between too much information and not enough?

Somewhere along the way, this got decided. Somewhere along the way, a general idea of what topics to include in a World History or US History course were decided, and it has remained pretty consistent since that nameless day when units were born and content christened.

But it's the same history now as then. Right?

It's also still limited, narrow in scope, shaping our students' understanding and excluding youthful interests.

Imagine a World History text without the unit "The Age of Revolution" or "The Scientific Revolution" or the "Industrial Revolution" or whatever other event got the label revolution stamped on it at some point.

We've come to accept these textbook units as God-given. Heck, what other units could there be?

Tons.

CHOICE

That's where you and your class come in. Build a custom text.

An enormous amount of easily accessible information exists today. Traditionally, textbooks served as the sole source of information students needed for a course. A tradition outdated.

Many of the teachers today remember years at school without the Internet, without easy access to information. Their textbooks were the information, little else. We once went to the encyclopedias in our house to write reports on amphibians, copying the information straight to our notebooks. Mission accomplished.

Our students don't suffer the same limits on information, so we shouldn't make them suffer book-report-preparing texts.

Our students have the ability to do so much more.

We don't want our students copying information from a single source. We want them to pull from multiple sources and synthesize that information into a convincing theory.

Then, if we are going to put so much power into the hands of the students, where the students investigate their own sources, why not let the students choose their own topics. Let them write the textbook.

What a wild semester project and summative assessment this could be. Throughout the semester, the course could follow the required curriculum, but with each unit, students could investigate the *missing links* or dive deeper into a topic they thought didn't get the time it deserved. Wow! Accumulate these over the years, and you'd have quite the library.

Place the students in the driver's seat. Give them the opportunity to be curious, to create, and to imagine. Let the students complete a textbook's chapter.

Too difficult for high school students?

Not if you create the system.

How do you do that? Dr. Carol Dweck talks of a growth mindset, where students own their success—they're in the driver's seat.

The brain has to struggle through challenging workouts, just as a football player in a gym has to do in order to build muscle so he can make the play come game time. Dweck refers to this as grit. Students need to build grit, and grit enables students to brush themselves off and try harder when they've just been smacked with a task they find difficult.

It's important, as Dweck writes, to talk with the students about a growth mindset and that you value progress. During the course of the year, it's important to build a classroom that values effort and investigation, more so than points and A+ scores.

For the purposes here, let's devise a student-created text that stresses connectivity, cause and effect, and the chronology of events. Give the students a template for a book where each chapter is identified by only a date, 1650, for example. Students take on the challenge of discovering what occurred in that year around the globe. The next chapter could be 1750, all the way to 2050, where they make some predictions based on evidence they cite.

Traditionally, students would get the impacts of the English civil war story or the repercussions of Luther's protest, but would they get the Mughal-Safavid War, where Afghanistan, as usual, is fought over? Perhaps this would be of some interest to students, and you could definitely make the relevant connection to modern struggles in Afghanistan.

Or students could venture westward, where they might discover the French meeting with the Erie as they embarked across what would become Ohio. Students would uncover a world of Iroquois and Huron people, giving some identity to the rather generic Cleveland Major League nickname, the Indians.

The entire semester is a collection of students' work that complements the regular curriculum. A piece of each unit's assessment would include the book the students are writing. Too difficult to grade with constructive feedback? Possibly. But if you feel that way, group students up to tackle their chosen chapters, which builds communication skills that require students to articulate their thoughts, and articulating thoughts gets that brain manipulating ideas in the head, like pumping iron at the gym.

How might this look?

BUILDING GROUPS AND GIVING THEM A GOAL

In a class of twenty-nine students, divide the students into seven groups of four, with one group at five. These are rotating groups, so that no one group is the same for the, let's say, seven units.

The units will be divided by regions: 1. North Africa, 2. East Asia, 3. Indian subcontinent, 4. West Africa, 5. North America, 6. South America, 7. Europe.

The group with five students would take on the task of Europe. Since Europe is already part of the curriculum, you could challenge this group to identify a topic in Europe that was either ignored or glossed over in the regular text—an event or person the students feel should have been given more time. There are five in their group, so they have to do a little extra and explain to the class why this topic maybe wasn't given the same amount of airplay in the textbook as other topics. This is something they could turn into a news story or dramatization.

Each group has to develop an activity for their chapter—make them build the lesson. On top of writing the chapter on their topic, they'll have to include, as all textbooks do, additional activities. Some ideas may include exercises on differentiation, beyond the classroom activities to extend the lesson, articles students can read or films they can watch to learn more, plus a section where students have to debate a topic.

Ask the students to be informative. Students should include specific examples and stories. To help student groups develop an angle, ask them to look at topics from different perspectives or lenses. Tell students to consider looking at their topic through one of the following, using the skills listed in chapter 10.

Stress focus and depth. Students should look for a story, one that they would enjoy and find interesting. This might take some practice. Students have been conditioned to write some pretty boring reports that no employer would like to read. Take a few days to read some creative history, watch some, and then practice writing some. Students can read their creative history pieces to the class. Does it entertain the class?

Once students identify a particular person or event in history that they could turn into a good story, ask them to take it a step further. Talk about the person's intention and impact, for instance. Get into their head. In Dr. Carol Dweck's *Mindset: The New Psychology of Success*, she describes how the brain is designed to seek things out. Ask students to seek and explain why they believe the historical character they are writing about thought such a way.

Some guiding themes could be: 1. Government, 2. Economics, 3. Religion, 4. Culture and Fashion, 5. Sports and Entertainment, 6. Visual and Performing Arts, 7. Education, 8. War and Peace, 9. Science and Math, 10. Rebels. Students could choose a theme from this list to help them focus their investigation.

In the end, compile the students' chapters over the semester and turn it into something like *The Other World History* or *History Through Our Interests*.

TURNING THE BLAND INTO SOMETHING SPICY

This takes some skill and definitely practice. It takes practice turning bland, factual information into something that reads like a story.

Practice with a picture. Give the students a visual aid and ask them to write a story about it. Ask them to write about what happened prior to the moment the picture was taken, or what happened as a result. What is the person in the picture thinking?

The next step is to keep the picture description in historical context. If the picture is Andrew Jackson sitting on his horse, Sam Patch, then the students will have to include events surrounding Jackson's life if they want to be right about what might be going through Old Hickory's head.

Such research and storytelling builds students' critical-thinking skills. It enhances their ability to apply their research, to discriminate between information that can be used and information that can't, and to think creatively, weeding all of their robot tendencies out. *Telling True Stories* by Mark Kramer is a great resource for strategies on writing creative nonfiction. Pick it up and get inspired.

Kramer provides and explains a list of strategies for building a narrative that attracts the reader. It would be worth it for your students to read this short list. In the quickest of all sums, students need to intrigue the readers with not just the topic but the emotions surrounding that topic. What would you see or hear or smell or feel if you stood on the battlefield at Gettysburg? And the scenes students write can't just sit still. There needs to be action and a point to that action. The readers need to be lured in and want to stay with the story, and this can only be done through extensive research.

Of course, much of what the students read in history classes is rather drab and dry snapshots of moments in history. If students read boring history, they'll regurgitate boring history.

Try introducing students to some historic fiction so that they get a more colorful image of history. If you can't find a book that complements the class or fits the timeframe, take a look at some graphic novels, many of which beautifully illustrate adventures in history.

Reading an exciting account of an event in history will assist the students in understanding how to turn their research into something engaging to read.

Oh, about reading . . .

David Giffels teaches creative writing at the University of Akron. He was kind enough to lend some advice:

> The only way to be an excellent writer is to first be an excellent reader, and second, to write. It really is that simple. And that complicated. Many young people who want to write creatively aren't as engaged with the wholeness of literature as they ought to be. I always return a statement I once heard from the music producer Quincy Jones, who said that becoming an artist is the process of imitating your idols until you sound like yourself. Most writers go through a long process of discovering their inspirations, then channeling those writers' styles, until they emerge with a style of their own. I know it has been, and continues to be this way for me.

So, get those kids to read, but get them to read the right stuff, not the boring stuff. Leave that for us teachers.

A little something on depth. Depth pulls readers in. Depth gives emotion to a reading. Depth opens the door to perspectives and debate. Depth makes us want to know more.

Kids like to know why things happen, or are, or this, or that. At a young age, kids ask *why* all the time, for everything. They're curious.

The world is totally expansive. It's everything. Young kids see this, and they ask, "Why is the sky blue?" or "Why do we eat goats but not doggies?" Kids want to take the visual a bit further.

Then kids get to school, and they are once again fed everything—breadth. Few *whys* are answered with breadth. Social Studies courses become an overview.

But it's a survey course. This is true. But where is the balance between *giving students an overview* and *losing students in the process*?

We need to leave time in our classes for the *why*.

Let the students decide what that *why* is.

Textbooks can be lengthy and dry, losing students from the get-go.

There's no point in the length of the history texts. If their job is to give an overview, then give an overview and be done with it. Leave it up to the students to investigate further.

Textbooks should not be the only resource for students. They shouldn't even be the bulk of the information for students. In the real world, students will have to consult multiple sources in order to develop a well-rounded solution.

An ideal text would be one that devotes a couple pages to each chapter. Part of the chapter could include a story to lure the students into the content. The rest of the chapter could summarize the main jist of the chapter, highlighting key words and characters.

Textbooks read like droning robots. There's very little charisma in a textbook.

Writing your own textbook allows you to use your own voice, something that will sound familiar to students between reading and at home and discussions in class. Something else that throws off students is the wording—it's not in your words, it's in bland words.

So, to reiterate, we want a history textbook that:

1. Is short in length.
2. Reads in your voice.
3. Holds the reader's attention.

Find a history text with these characteristics. You won't.

This is the perfect opportunity for you to write your own text, in your own voice, giving students a base to work from. Write a text with some humor, with some stories—something to keep the readers' attentions. Each unit is a few pages, highlighting the big ideas. Leave the students wondering what's next with clever essential questions.

Include maps drawn by you, and make them interactive. Include pictures you've taken. If you've seen World War II sites in France, include that story with pictures.

Take a summer and write your own quick guide to world history that can be used as a resource to get each unit off the ground.

If you feel that writing a text is too much on your own, bring your Social Studies department on board and divvy up the work. Just be sure that everyone involved understands the concept and keeps a similar voice—you don't want one chapter to be colorful and attention-grabbing and the next just drab.

It isn't too hard to publish your own book. There are several free online sources, like CreateSpace, you can use. Put it on Amazon if you'd like. Or, if you want your text interactive, publish your book onto iTunes so that students can download it for free onto their device.

If you or your department goes through the work of writing the book, you might as well publish it. Similarly, if your students do all that hard work, publish it. Students will get a kick out of seeing their work on Amazon.

DEAD WEIGHT

During their professional career, students will not be handed a book that includes all of the answers for the job. Rather, employers will be expecting their employees to develop the answers to problems.

Textbooks are restrictive, boring, and downright dead weight.

Textbooks are restrictive because they become a crutch. It's where students go for answers. This once served a purpose. But this was limiting, just as the single paragraph on the U.S. intervention in Guatemala in 1954 current World History texts.

Textbooks are boring because they have to be. They're cumbersome and broad in order to address all of the topics. Textbooks have no personality—one colorless story after another. Even when they're biased they don't know they're biased.

Textbooks are heavy. Students carry around all the chapters throughout all of the year.

Of course, there are some positives.

Textbook companies are changing, no doubt. They're creating interactive ebooks that can update information.

Textbooks provide students with a guide. If a kid didn't quite get something in class, she can refer to her textbook to clear the confusion.

Textbooks divide history into organized headings, chapters, and units.

Let's set aside the textbook for a moment. Let's go textbookless. Tell the kids, "Off you go. Research it."

Well, that'll be a mess.

There's just so much information out there for the students. Kids will come back the next day claiming to be "so confused."

There has to be a middle ground between traditional textbooks and everything on the Internet. Students need some freedom, but they definitely need some guidance too.

As a history teacher, you know the content, each chapter, and the interesting narratives that draw in the students. Each year, you cover notes that are probably in the form of a presentation. Why not turn that presentation into a short book to be used as the students' main text? You can include the basics, but in your own language, one that sounds like the language used in class. In your short book, you can include interesting anecdotes that give some color to the content.

Your text can be used as an introductory reading for each chapter, giving students an overview of the chapter. Include keywords that would otherwise be given to them as a vocab assignment. Include a page of essential questions for your book's content and beyond.

- Include websites in your book as extended readings.
- Include links to your website that lead to extended readings.
- Include questions to be discussed on your class learning management system.
- Include links to specific webpages of events and people you want to emphasize.

If it's your ebook, you can edit it at will. If a website you link to changes, you can make the adjustment. To keep current, include current events or topics to act as extended readings.

Include pictures, maps, interactive visuals, or videos of you commenting on an historic event.

Give your book the flare your textbooks never had. This is a generation that demands speed and pizzazz. Don't disappoint them with shorter versions of the same old textbook.

Use your textbook as an opportunity to excite. Take a summer and write two-page chapters that summarize the gist of the main idea. It won't be complete. You complete the story by linking to a website, or ask your students to complete it.

For instance, if the unit is on the Indian Subcontinent, include an introduction to the Holi (Festival of Color) and link to National Geographic's website, where there are beautiful pictures of the Hindu holiday.

Provide a short explanation of Hinduism, including keywords like dharma and karma, and then link to a site that nicely illustrates and explains the gods of Hinduism.

Link to a video of an Indian public service commercial to change men's attitude toward women, and include supplementary readings to further that content.

The point is, all the information is online, it's just up to you to choose what pages to include to best motivate your students and help them understand the content. A traditional textbook isn't necessary. An e-text isn't necessary. You know all the information the students are required to learn. Do yourself a favor, and collect all of your notes and presentations into a book to be used by your students.

In truth, a textbook could be a series of websites and questions chosen by you and your department. The guiding questions matter the most. Then it's up to you to decide the best sources online that will answer those questions. No textbook necessary.

HMMM, THAT SOUNDS INTERESTING

Here's a bit of a taste of what your textbook could look like:

Muhammad ibn Musa al-Khwarizmi sits by a lamp that illuminates his scribbling of equations in Baghdad's House of Wisdom, so called because of its collection of scholars from Greece to India. Al-Khwarizmi draws a circle into his equation. The circle is a zero, unknown to the West, and borrowed from Indian scholars to the East. Al-Khwarizmi pauses for a moment, looking to the flickering candle at his side for inspiration. He sits on an ornately decorated rug in a room lined with books and pointed archways. He can hear the comfort of the fountain in the courtyard.

As a cross-roads, Baghdad benefitted from a mixing of ideas that would help al-Khwarizmi develop what we call algebra, which is the Latinized version of the Arab word *al-jabar*. Calculate that.

By AD 800, the Abbasid Caliphate ruled the Islamic empire of the Middle East. They established their capital in Baghdad, a nicely positioned city along the trade routes from east to west. Along this route, the invention of paper would make its way to Baghdad by the eighth century, which made collecting documents much easier and less expensive. Unlike Europe where the Catholic Church dictated science, Islam welcomed the brains of Christians, Jews, and Hindus.

A welcoming attitude and an advantageous location allowed Baghdad to thrive. For instance, through the use and study of Hindu texts and the scholars who could translate Sanskrit, the concept of zero and decimals made their way to Baghdad, which helped progress math and science tremendously. Keep in mind, the Roman Empire had a lot, but it didn't have a zero Roman numeral. Think about it.

The intelligence of Iraq during this period greatly influenced later periods. For instance, the scholar Alhazen who made discoveries in optics would lead the English philosopher Roger Bacon to cite his work. Alhazen also influenced the philosopher Averroes, who lived in Spain during the 1100s, and who used Alhazen's wisdom to help him make breakthroughs in science that Johannes Kepler would later call "inertia."

Unlike Europe, the Middle East was united during the European Middle Ages. How would unity help bring progress as opposed to the divided environment of Europe?

CLOSING THOUGHT

Don't feel like writing a text to accompanying a course? Film an introductory video for each unit.

A bit on teacher videos: these need to be short and to the point. If students won't read more than 140 characters, then they won't watch a video over two minutes.

1. Script your video.
2. One per unit.
3. Jazz it up. Choose a setting. Invite a guest speaker.
4. Include animations, such as keywords on the screen or maps.
5. Videos should be extenders, no fillers.

NOTE

1. I remember when my department got the newest edition of Prentice Hall's *World Cultures: A Global Mosaic*. It, like its older predecessor, included the same picture of Sunny Ade in the music section on Africa and a half-column of text accompany the picture. The text names Ade and Fela Kuti, describing both in a seven-line paragraph. How can you take these colorful, influential, dynamic people and make something interesting out of them in seven lines? A haiku would have been more respectful.

Conclusion: A Social Studies Course for Social Studies' Sake

Okay, let's wrap this whole thing up.

One more time, what do we want our students to gain from a Social Studies course? Facts? More like, how to *utilize* facts. Facts can be used to support a position, but before the facts are useful, a student needs to learn how to think, how to put those facts to use.

The purpose of a social studies course, such as history, is to enhance critical thinking. How do we do this? What does the data say? Data-driven decision-making is all the rage. The business world has been obsessed with the collection of data for a long time, and No Child Left Behind introduced the world of education to the wonders of data.

However, too much of a reliance on data can be worrisome. When students turn into numbers in a spreadsheet, we run the risk of missing the importance of the personal one on one, the importance of humanity.

But data is here to stay. So, what does the data say?

1. Data tells us that rested students learn better. Some schools are adopting late starts since the data shows that high-school-aged students need many more hours than their teachers. A late start, whether it's once a week or every day, injects some energy into the school, and thus the classroom, so says a study done by the University of Minnesota in 2014. Not to mention, more sleep means less stress. But if schools are not willing to start later, how else can teachers inject some energy? How else can we "change it up"?

2. Data tells us students who are free from the constraints of sitting for hours learn better. Some schools are welcoming standing desks, and it makes sense. When students can move around, their brains are invigo-

rated. In a story posted on Today.com in October 2015, students talk about the joys of standing desks. Moving helps the kids keep from "spacing out," and, added bonus, the data apparently shows a jump in test scores.

3. Data tells us that giving students a role in the classroom increases motivation. Students who can choose what to study feel more competent in their studies. In an article written by Janelle Cox, titled "Crafting Effective Choices to Motivate Students," she talks about a sense of purpose and how "the more meaningful an activity is to the person engaging in it, the more likely he or she will be motivated to continue doing it."

4. Data shows that learning by doing is long-term learning. Students who have the opportunity to engage with their subject, discovering on their own, develop a deeper understanding. As David Kolb stated in his 1984 article, "Experiential Learning," that learning is about creating knowledge. And his findings didn't change much thirty years later in his book on experiential learning, as he states that experiential learning "links education, work, and personal development."

Given the data, education should be much more active and mobile and self-led, not restricted to our traditional early bird school mornings that throw class after class at students, as the poor kids move from room to room, sitting and sitting, stressing and stressing.

If we believe in allowing the data to guide us, shouldn't we make large-scale adjustments to the aging system of education?

Some schools have put these ideas into practice, and we see good things happening, but it's doubtful that these changes will occur on a widespread scale anytime soon. However, in the short term and on a smaller scale, consider what these adjustments would look like. Think of making baby-step changes. Adjust from the bottom up, one class at a time.

Consider creating a single course that embodies the philosophy of an active class that engages with a subject chosen by each student.

How can we allow the students to interact with their history? How can we allow the students some choice and autonomy with their history? How can we help our students become experts in history? How can we make it so that the students can touch, see, and smell their history?

Local history.

We spend a lot of time in school teaching students history of far-off lands and eras. Students feel disconnected from these worlds. There's a lack of relevance. "How does this apply to me?" students ask their brains. "It doesn't," the brains answer back.

A study of the students' immediate world would serve them better. There's history wherever we go. Why not start with the self and then move to the abstract beyond? If students see a connection between their daily commute to school and the content being discussed in class, there will be more buy-in. If students realize a bridge between the school world and their real life, they won't feel so distant from the content. If students feel their background and neighborhood is important, then they'll have an interest and maybe even participate.

Local history is powerful. Local culture is powerful. The students can't help but feel a connection to the content. But a study of local history will be different everywhere, so how would that work with the standards?

Again, if we focus on the *skills* instead of the content, which seems more useful in the twenty-first century, it doesn't matter what the history is. A study of New York City will no doubt be different and possibly include a more abundant number of resources than a study of Wichita.

How do we accommodate for this?

No doubt, the history and culture from city to city will be different, but to think that one city has a richer past than another is totally off the mark. Not to mention, there are many different ways to examine a single place.

Let's consider an example of what a course on local history would look like.

Which city can we use as an example? Perhaps a mid-sized, midwestern city. An "average" city. How about Akron, Ohio?

A course on the relatively unknown Akron, Ohio, could be a semester course, where the goal for the students is specifically to engage. Engage with the community. Engage the brain. Engage responsibility. The course content could be split between the first quarter and the second.

The first quarter could focus primarily on the history of Akron, sprinkling current event discussions throughout. The second quarter could focus more on current events and current questions the city is grappling with. There's no textbook necessarily on Akron, Ohio, so where would the students get their information?

Most cities don't have a textbook, but there are plenty of sources to pull from, everything from local authors to newspapers to the library's historical documents to pamphlets printed by historic sites or historical societies.

And where the documents lack, tap into the genius of historians. The best part about studying a hometown is the easy access and willingness of guest speakers. Use the local experts as the textbook. They're a textbook that can take questions in real time! Without technology!

It takes a little work on the front end to meet with local experts in order to figure out how they could fit into the class, but think about how rich it would be to bring an expert in each week. Together, the teacher and the local experts could build the curriculum, bridging the sometimes disappointing gap between education and the real world.

In the meantime, the teacher can find a variety of print sources for the students to read—short, specific readings about the hometown that don't mess around with the vagueness and insincere voice of a bulky textbook. All the while, the students could be compiling information to build their own textbook, citing local experts to support their information.

It takes little effort anymore to self-publish a book. There are plenty of online sites that assist with this and make it quite simple for the user. Or perhaps, the local university would be willing to take on the project and help with the publishing.

Teach the students collaboration, not by telling them but by engaging with the community. Break through those walls that make education seem like something separate from the outside world. What the students should be learning in class should prepare them for that outside world, not hide them or protect them from it.

A course on Akron could invite experts on the native Seneca populations and the use of the Cuyahoga River. The next speaker could talk about the canal system that would bring the city to life. Another speaker could talk about the oats and marble industries of the 1800s. The next speaker could talk about how the city became the Rubber Capital of the world. The final speaker on history could talk about the modern struggles of a "Rust Belt" city.

If speakers can't be found for every unit, gather supplementary readings for the students. The local library, museum, or university could be of assistance here. Utilize those community resources. It doesn't matter the city, town, or village. There is history and culture to study. With a population of just over 1,500, Lusk, Wyoming, boasts a rich history of the Wild West and plenty of resources, such as the Niobrara Library and its abundant archives.

Link your city's history with other similar cities to build a broader story if you feel it's necessary. As a Rust Belt city, Akron's twentieth century shares a common story with cities like St. Louis, Detroit, Pittsburgh, Buffalo, and Cleveland. The group just so happens to star in the documentary *Red, White, and Blueprint*. If there's no documentary on your town's history, pair up with the school's art teacher or the local library's audio-visual department and give the job of making a documentary to your students.

Call those students to action!

Ask students to venture out into the community to observe their surroundings, old buildings, and historic markers, for example. Have the students take pictures. Post the pictures on social media. Post the pictures on a student website where they collect all of their findings. Build a collection of pictures and student reflections. Organize an end-of-semester presentation at the school, where the students teach an audience of the community about their hometown, using references from experts and the pictures.

There are an endless number of directions a teacher and school could take a local history course.

The second quarter would examine the culture of the city, including neighborhoods, music and entertainment, arts, religion, and highlighted attractions. In the same quarter, the class would cover the current state of the city's responsibilities, such as education, public safety, neighborhoods, health, law, police and fire, and whatever else you'd like to include. Contact the city to see if members of city council would be willing to get involved. There's model UN, why not model city council?

The topics of the proposed second quarter make it all the easier to engage with the community. Bring a police officer to talk to the class about building relationships between the police and neighborhoods. Invite an expert on city planning and the city's infrastructure. Bring some people in from the art museum to talk about the value the arts play in the community. The head of the city library's special collections could talk with the students about how to use the collection.

Require a group of students to spend ten minutes with each guest, interviewing them while on camera. The footage could be used for a class project, as well as for next year's class as a resource. And with each speaker, build an activity that asks the students to put the expert's presentations into action.

If someone talks to the class about what to do with abandoned houses or old buildings, challenge your class to develop plans. Ask students to research what other cities have done with abandoned houses and old buildings that have succeeded (or failed). Ask students to identify articles that address the topic, either locally or in another similar city (in the case of Akron, another Rust Belt city).

In a local history class, students should be required to complete assignments that include engaging with the community. Teachers can ask students to collect several first-hand accounts of historical sites with the goal of building a portfolio of sites. Take Akron, for instance, which still has remnants of the Ohio-Erie Canal. On their own time, students could venture with a group of friends to a canal spot and take pictures and read about the canal and post it on their website portfolio.

Have a little fun with "on-site assignments." Organize several walking tours of your city. Hold them after school. Any student who wants to participate can join you, fulfilling one of their on-site requirements. Walking tours allow teachers to take learning beyond the classroom. The learning experience becomes real. Students get to see the history first hand, even touch the history. Teachers can show how the past merges with the present by identifying where buildings once were or how older buildings stand next to newer, underscoring the importance of city planning.

A Social Studies course that allows the students to examine their surroundings, first, shows students how to engage in their community, and second, allows students to practice their civic skills first hand.

Consider a course that focuses on your hometown, not at the fourth-grade level but at the high school level. In the course you could:

1. Ask students to build a website where they store their work.
2. Give students a list of assignments that they will complete and post on their website, including reflections, pictures from around the city, interviews of local experts, and solutions to questions the city is dealing with.
3. Have each student choose and complete an independent study.
4. Invite experts from the community to the classroom to address real-life situations relevant to the students' lives.
5. Organize field trips to local historical spots. These field trips could be during school or after school. They could be mandatory or optional. Lead a walking tour of your hometown, showing students real-life examples of topics discussed in class.
6. Create a curriculum that actually includes the students. They live in the subject of study and thus are an active member in what they are studying.

Visionary and author Roger Schank busies himself with how to make school less horrible. He states in his book, *Teaching Minds*, "Real knowledge is acquired as a natural part of a cognitive process in service of a goal."

In his blog, *Education Outrage*, Schrank talks about creating experiences that simulate the real world. Rather than delivering information, provide opportunities to experience what it is you want the students to do, such as problem solve.

Bottom line, is it best for the students?

- Are the decisions you're making for your lessons directly assisting the success of your students for the future?
- Are you challenging students to think beyond memorization?
- Are you giving students the tools necessary to see events from multiple perspectives?
- Are you providing students with real life learning opportunities?
- Are you placing students in active and engaging situations?
- Are you allowing students time to reflect on what they have learned?

- Are you teaching students to embrace the process more than the points?
- Are you putting the students in the driver seats? (Manual or automatic?)
- Are you placing students in contact with active members of the community?
- Are you encouraging students to build, create, and innovate as a means of assessment?
- Are you testing the status quo, pushing the barriers?
- Are you leading your school in a direction that opens up the four walls of a classroom?
- Are you excited?

CLOSING THOUGHT

It's not easy. There's not always time. It isn't always appreciated. It doesn't always work. But do your best to look at the Social Studies through a different lens or new light or from another discipline. Take the pgEd Project, for instance. The mission is "to increase awareness and conversation about the benefits and ethical, legal, and social implications of personal genetics." In order to fulfill their mission, they build lessons for many subject areas, including Social Studies. How the heck can a history teacher make genetics relevant for the students—or vibrant for that matter? There are great deliberations students can engage in regarding the history of eugenics, from Plato to the U.S. Immigration Act of 1924. Students can also take on the discussion surrounding what role one's DNA can play, for good or bad.

Bibliography

Barber, N. (2014, October 2). Focus on the Process and Results Will Follow. Retrieved July 7, 2016, from Edutopia website: http://www.edutopia.org/blog/ focus-process-results-will-follow-nathan-barber.

Cohen, P. (2016, February 23). The Problem with High School Nostalgia. Retrieved June 29, 2016, from U.S. News and World Report website: http://www.usnews.com/opinion/knowledge-bank/articles/2016-02-23/overhaul-high-school-to-better-prepare-students-for-their-futures.

Costa, A. L., & Kallick, B. (Eds.). (2009). *Learning and Leading with Habits of Mind.* Alexandria, VA: ASCD.

Dawn, R. (2015, October 23). Why Schools Are Adding Standing Desks to the Classroom. Retrieved July 10, 2016, from Today website: http://www.today.com/parents/why-schools-are-adding-standing-desks-classroom-t51856.

Dweck, C. S., Dr. (2007). *Mindset: The New Psychology of Success* (Reprint ed.). New York, NY: Ballantine Books.

Giffels, D. (2016, July 25). Personal interview.

Gregory, G., & Kaufeldt, M. (n.d.). The Motivated Brain: Improving Student Attention, Engagement, and Perseverance. Retrieved July 5, 2016, from ASCD website: http://www.ascd.org/publications/books/115041.aspx.

Groves, R., & Welsh, B. (2010). The High School Experience: What Students Say. Issues in *Educational Research*, 20(2), 87–104.

Hancock, L. (2011, September). Why are Finland's Schools Successful [Blog post]. Retrieved from Smithsonian.com website: http://www.smithsonianmag.com/innovation/why-are-finlands-schools-successful-49859555/.

How to Motivate Students Through Choice. (n.d.). Retrieved July 10, 2016, from TeachHUB.com website: http://www.teachhub.com/how-motivate-students-through-choice.

Hull, J., & Newport, M. (2011, December). Time in School: How Does the U.S. Compare? [Fact sheet]. Retrieved July, 2016, from Center for Public Education website: http://www.centerforpubliceducation.org/Main-Menu/Organizing-a-school/Time-in-school-How-does-the-US-compare.

Kamenetz, A. (2016, February 24). High School 'Work from Home Day' Gives Students Taste of Independence [Blog post]. Retrieved from KQED News website: http://ww2.kqed.org/mindshift/2016/02/24/high-school-work-from-home-day-gives-students-taste-of-independence/.

Kolb, D. (1984). *Experiential Learning: Experience as the Source of Learning and Development.* Upper Saddle River, NJ: Prentice Hall.

Koloc, N. (2014). Let Employees Choose When, Where, and How to Work. *Harvard Business Review*. Retrieved from https://hbr.org/2014/11/let-employees-choose-when-where-and-how-to-work.

Kramer, M., & Call, W. (Eds.). (2007). *Telling True Stories: A Nonfiction Writers' Guide*. New York, NY: Plume.

Leveille, D. (Writer). (2016, February 4). A Young Pakistani Woman Hopes Her Soul-Searching Motorcycle Trip Will Inspire Others [Radio episode]. PRI's The World.

Medina, J. (Ed.). (2014). Brain Rules: 12 Principles for Surviving and Thriving at Work, Home, and School (2nd ed.). *National Curriculum Standards for Social Studies*: Chapter 2—The Themes of Social Studies [Fact sheet]. (n.d.). Retrieved July 6, 2016, from NCSS website: http://www.socialstudies.org/standards/strands.

National Standards for Social Studies Teachers. (2002). Silver Spring, MD: National Council for the Social Studies.

Orlin, B. (2013, September 9). When Memorization Gets in the Way of Learning. Retrieved June 23, 2016, from *The Atlantic* website: http://www.theatlantic.com/education/archive/2013/09/when-memorization-gets-in-the-way-of-learning/279425/.

Our Mission [Fact sheet]. (n.d.). Retrieved July 14, 2016, from Personal Genetics Education Project website: http://www.pged.org/mission/.

Project Soapbox/American Soapbox Initiative (n.d.). Retrieved July 5, 2016, from Mikva Challenge website: http://www.mikvachallenge.org/educators/online-resources/issues/project-soapbox/.

Ranzetta, T. (2016, January 18). Want to Set-up a Student-Run Coffee Shop? Here Are Schools to Contact! Retrieved July 5, 2016, from Next Gen Personal Finance website: http://nextgenpersonalfinance.org/want-to-set-up-student-run-coffee-shop-here-are-schools-to-contact/.

Schank, R. (2011). *Teaching Minds: How Cognitive Science Can Save Our Schools*. New York, NY: Teachers College Press.

Teale, W. H., & Gambrell, L. B. (2007). Raising Urban Students' Literacy Achievement by Engaging in Authentic, Challenging Work. *The Reading Teacher*, *60*(8), 728–39.

The Benefits of a Late Start. (2014, March 14). Retrieved July 10, 2016, from Discover, University of Minnesota website: http://discover.umn.edu/news/teaching-education/Late-start-times-benefit-high-school-students.

Weingarten, R., and Litow, S. (2015, December 18). On the Path to the Middle Class. Retrieved May 23, 2016, from *U.S. News and World Report* website: http://www.usnews.com/opinion/articles/2015-12-18/career-and-technical-education-programs-provide-path-to-middle-class-jobs.

Wiggins, G. (2014, May 30). Students Learn Best When You Do This. And This. And This. [Blog post]. Retrieved from *Teach Thought* website: http://www.teachthought.com/pedagogy/students-learn-best/.

Index

About the Author

Greg Milo has taught high school Social Studies for thirteen years. He currently works with Global Ties Akron and serves on the board of Akron Promise in Akron, Ohio. His goal is to design real-life and relevant experiential learning opportunities for students. As a result, he cofounded Project HOPE, a program where students hang out in the alleys, woods, and railroad tracks with the homeless of Akron, Ohio. Milo wrote about a night in the life of Project HOPE in *The Akron Anthology* by Belt Publishing.

The author has also organized overseas experiences to Kosovo, Poland, the Czech Republic, Germany, and France, where the students learned firsthand from government officials, NGO representatives, school teachers and principals, minority groups, and the everyday local citizen.

Milo has presented workshops to young teachers and at conventions and has been published in *Education Week*, *The Akronist*, and the *Devil Strip*. He can also be found at mrgregmilo.com, mrgregmilo on Instagram, and @Mr_Greg_Milo on Twitter.

In his spare time, Milo teaches people about healthy eating. As Working Class Vegan Man, he conducts cooking demonstrations and information sessions on how healthy eating is cool eating.